Islam: The Basics

Introducing Islam

ISLAM: The Basics

Kim Whitehead

Produced by OTTN Publishing, Stockton, New Jersey

Mason Crest Publishers
370 Reed Road
Broomall, PA 19008
www.masoncrest.com

3 5 7 9 8 6 4

Library of Congress Cataloging-in-Publication Data

Whitehead, Kim.
  Islam: the basics / Kim Whitehead.
      v. cm. — (Introducing Islam)
  Includes bibliographical references and index.
  Contents: Islam's role in the world — Allah's final prophet — Central beliefs —
  Islam divided: the major and minor sects — Law and practice — Islamic
  celebrations — Issues in contemporary Islam.
    ISBN 1-59084-697-4
  1. Islam—Juvenile literature. 2. Islam—Essence, genius, nature—Juvenile
  literature. 3. Islam—Doctrines—Juvenile literature. [1. Islam.] I. Title.
  II. Series.
    BP161.3.W47 2004
    297—dc22
                              2003013262

Contents

Introduction

The central belief of Islam, one of the world's major religions, is contained in a simple but powerful phrase: "There is no god but Allah, and Muhammad is his prophet." The Islamic faith, which emerged from the Arabian desert in the seventh century C.E., has become one of the world's most important and influential religions.

Within a century after the death of the Prophet Muhammad, Islam had spread throughout the Arabian Peninsula into Europe, Africa, and Asia. Today, Islam is the world's fastest-growing religion and Muslims can be found throughout the globe. There are about 1.25 billion Muslims, which means that approximately one of every five people follows Islam. The global total of believers has surpassed two older religions, Hinduism and Buddhism; only Christianity has more followers.

Muslims can also be found in North America. Many Muslims have immigrated to the United States and Canada, and large numbers of people—particularly African Americans—have converted to Islam since the 1960s. Today, there are an estimated 6 million Muslims in the United States, with an additional half-million Muslims in Canada.

Despite this growing popularity, many people in the West are uninformed about Islam. For many Americans, their only exposure to this important religion, with its glorious history and rich culture, is through news reports about wars in Muslim countries, terrorist attacks, or fundamentalist denunciations of Western corruption.

The purpose of the INTRODUCING ISLAM series is to provide an objective examination of Islam and give an overview of what Muslims believe, how they practice their faith, and what values they hold most important. Four volumes in particular focus on Islamic beliefs and religious practices. *Islam: The Basics* answers the essential questions about the faith and provides information about the major sects. *Islam, Christianity, Judaism* describes and explains the similarities and differences between these three great monotheistic religions. *Heroes and Holy Places* gives information about such important figures as Muhammad and Saladin, as well as shrines like Mecca and Jerusalem. *Islamic Fundamentalism* focuses on the emergence of the Islamist movement during the 20th century, the development of an Islamist government in Iran, and the differences between Islamists and moderates in such countries as Algeria, Indonesia, and Egypt.

Two volumes in the series explore Islam in the United States, and the relationship between the Muslim world and the West. *The American Encounter with Islam* provides specific history about Muslims in North America from the 17th century until the present, and traces the development of uniquely American sects like the Nation of Islam. *Muslims and the West* attempts to put the encounter between two important civilizations in broader perspective from a historical point of view.

Recent statistical data is extensively provided in two volumes, in order to discuss life in the Muslim world. *Who Are the Muslims?* is a geopolitical survey that explores the many different cultures that can be found in the Muslim world, as well as the different types of Islamic governments. *What Muslims Think, and How They Live* uses information collected in a landmark survey of the Islamic world by the Gallup Organization, as well as other socioeconomic data, to examine Muslim attitudes toward a variety of questions and issues.

As we enter a new century, cultural and political tensions between Muslims and non-Muslims continue. Now more than ever, it is important for people to learn more about their neighbors of all faiths. It is only through education and tolerance that we will be able to build a new world in which fear and mistrust are replaced with brotherhood and peace.

An Asian Muslim kneels to pray. Islam is one of the world's three major monotheistic faiths, and followers of the religion, known as Muslims, can be found in every country.

Islam's Role in the World

Few images in world religion evoke as profound a sense of reverence as the sight of a Muslim who, upon hearing the call to prayer, stops whatever he or she is doing, rolls a prayer carpet on the floor or ground, and recites prayers to Allah (*Allah* is the Arabic word for God). This scene, which is repeated five times a day, is echoed in businesses, homes, schools, and in the calm of community mosques, where believers kneel side by side as they lower their foreheads to the floor and pray.

But other images of Islam also abound. In the tangle of contemporary international relations, non-Muslims with little exposure to Islam remain confused about who Muslims really are. What are their beliefs, and what values do they share in common with Jews and Christians? How do Muslims practice their faith in their everyday lives? Who are their leaders and what is the shape of their religious institutions? What beliefs and practices set the average Muslim apart from the militant extremists spoken of so often in the news?

MUSLIMS AROUND THE GLOBE

These questions become all the more important as the number of Muslims continues to increase rapidly. Islam is the fastest-growing religion in the world. Most estimates now put the worldwide Muslim population at about 1.25 billion people, which means that one out of every five humans is a Muslim. Islam has surpassed the older religions Hinduism and Buddhism to become the second-largest religion in the world; only Christianity, with about 33 percent of the global population, has more followers.

The founder of Islam, the Prophet Muhammad (d. 632 C.E.), first reported his revelations from Allah in the early seventh century. Within just a few decades, Muhammad's religious movement had attracted converts and consolidated power throughout his homeland, the Arabian Peninsula, which is located between Africa and Asia. Today, that heritage remains strong in the Arab countries of the Middle East, where 90 to 95 percent of citizens claim Islam as their faith.

But Islam never knew borders and Muslims believed Allah had commanded them to spread their faith. Within a century of Muhammad's death, Islam had spread into Europe, Africa, and Asia. Today most Muslims are not Arabs, and Islam is the dominant religion in many countries outside the Arabian Peninsula. The four countries with the highest numbers of Muslims among their citizens—Indonesia, Pakistan, Bangladesh, and India—are located in Asia, not the Middle East. In many countries of Africa and southern Asia, more than 50 percent of the population follows Islam. And millions of Muslims live in Western Europe and the United States, thanks to emigration from Muslim countries and increasing conversions among European and American citizens. In the United States, for example, the rate of conversion among African Americans has exploded since the 1960s.

ISLAM AMONG OTHER RELIGIONS

The word *Islam* comes from the Arabic verb *aslama*, which means "submitted." The word *Muslim* is also Arabic and refers to a person who submits to the will of Allah. Devout Muslims everywhere submit themselves to Allah daily, both through their faith and by following Islamic law and the commandments in their holy text, the *Qur'an*, which was revealed by Allah to the Prophet Muhammad. Muslims believe that Allah's will must be obeyed in every sphere of life, and that they will be eternally rewarded if they follow His commands. This dedication to Allah's will is visible in daily acts—prayer, cleanliness in word and deed, commitment to family.

Islam is the youngest of the major world religions, and its origins highlight the meshing of religions and cultures in that part of the world during the seventh century. Muslims believe the Prophet Muhammad was sent as a messenger to humanity in order to affirm and develop Allah's divine message, which had been partially revealed by earlier prophets. Muslims see Muhammad as the last prophet in a line that includes Abraham, a Biblical figure also revered by Jews and Christians, and such other patriarchs and prophets as Noah, Isaac, Ishmael, Moses, and Jesus. Islam, Judaism, and Christianity stand apart from other major religions because of their *monotheism*, or belief in a single god.

As cultural and political tensions between Muslims and non-Muslims continue into the 21st century, the shared origins of Islam, Christianity, and Judaism lend a growing sense of urgency to Westerners' task of learning more about Islam.

Allah's Final Prophet

As he approached his fortieth birthday, in the year
610, a man named Muhammad ibn Abd Allah left
his home in the oasis city of Makka (Mecca), on
the Arabian Peninsula, and made his way north to
Mount Hira. Every year, Muhammad spent time alone
in a cave on Mount Hira, where he prayed and fasted.
This year, however, Muhammad was troubled by the
state of affairs on the Arabian Peninsula. Around him
he saw growing spiritual confusion and an increasingly
materialistic culture that dismissed moral values.

Muhammad had been born in Mecca around the year
570. He was orphaned by the age of six and worked as
a shepherd under the protection of his uncle. As a young
man, Muhammad worked on caravans following the
trade routes between Arabia and Syria. During this time,
he probably met Jews, Christians, and *Zoroastrians*. The

prophets and scriptures of these religions offered their believers a stability and coherence that the *polytheistic* Arab cultures did not possess. At age 25 Muhammad married Khadija, a wealthy widow for whom he had worked as a business agent. As the years passed, Muhammad's reputation as a trustworthy man grew—he became known as al-Amin, "the trusted one"—but so did his doubts about the direction he saw his society taking.

At this time on the Arabian Peninsula, the central unit of social organization was the tribe, which included smaller groupings of related families known as clans. (Although many Arabs were pagans, there were also quite a few Christians, whose values supported the preservation of tribe and family but who also had a concept of a life after death.) In general, the values of Arabian society supported the preservation of tribe and family. The Arabs believed that proper behavior involved following the ways of their ancestors and preserving the honor of the tribe. Belonging to a tribe

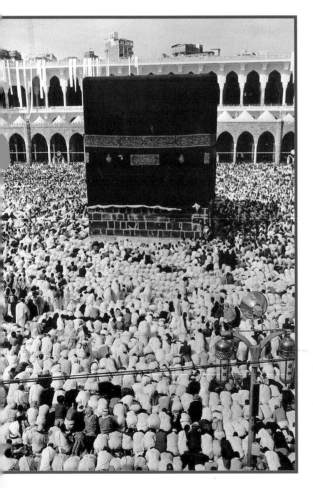

Thousands of Muslims kneel in prayer around the Kaaba, the black building that is the most sacred site in Islam. Muslims believe the Kaaba was built by Adam, the first man, as a place of worship.

also provided protection; though vendettas were common, the threat of inter-tribal bloodshed helped hold together a society without a single government or set of laws.

In the polytheistic religion of the peninsula, various gods and goddesses were viewed as guardians of individual tribes and were the objects of sacrifice, and prayer at local shrines. The nomadic Arabs carried small figurines representing gods and goddesses on their journeys, and they believed other helpful spirits lived in natural features like trees and springs. The Arabs asked their deities for guidance on all kinds of matters, from marriage arrangements to the mediation of disagreements. There was one holy place in which an Arab could worship all the gods and goddesses. This cube-shaped building in Mecca, known as the Kaaba, was the destination for a huge annual *pilgrimage*.

Beyond this collection of minor deities was the vague idea of a supreme, impersonal god known as Allah, who was uninvolved in day-to-day events. Allah was thought to provide rain and to seal agreements between tribes and individuals, but beyond this he was prayed to no more often than the lesser gods and goddesses.

Economic changes were occurring on the peninsula during Muhammad's lifetime. Increasing number of Arabs were leaving their nomadic ways and settling in urban centers. As a center of trade and commerce, Mecca was among the most prosperous oasis cities on the Arabian Peninsula. Life in the thriving cities brought new political and economic realities, in which the drive to accumulate wealth increasingly created disparity between rich and poor and threatened the system of moral values. Muhammad's own tribe, the Quraysh, had become rich through trading. The greed of tribal leaders and the hedonistic, materialistic, and immoral practices that plagued the society of Mecca concerned Muhammad.

It was during this period of inner turmoil and doubt about Arab society that Muhammad received his first revelation from Allah in the year 610 on the 27th night of the month of *Ramadan*. While Muhammad was sleeping in the cave on Mount Hira, something extraordinary happened: he was awakened by an overwhelming presence, which commanded, "Read!" When Muhammad stammered that he could not read, the command was repeated twice more. Muhammad responded each time that he could not read. Then, after suffering the feeling of being suffocated almost to death, he heard:

> "Read! In the name of your Lord, Who created, created man, out of a (mere) clot of congealed blood. Read! And your Lord is Most Bountiful, He Who taught by the Pen, taught man that which he knew not. (Qur'an 96: 1–5)

Muslims refer to the night of this first revelation to Muhammad as the Night of Power and Excellence. For the next 10 days, the Angel Gabriel taught Muhammad the message he should proclaim—that there was no god except Allah, and that all people should submit to the will of Allah. The revelations Muhammad received were eventually recorded in the Qur'an.

THE EARLY DAYS OF ISLAM

Soon after Muhammad received the first revelations, he began preaching Allah's message to small groups of people. However, he was afraid of persecution, so for the first three years much of his preaching was done in secret. Still, his followers had grown into a core group of committed converts, including his wife Khadija (d. 619), his kinsman Abu Bakr (d. 634), and his cousin Ali (d. 661), the son of the uncle who had cared for Muhammad as a boy. In 613, Muhammad began preaching the faith in Mecca openly and publicly.

Muhammad strongly condemned the immorality of Meccan society, and its unjust and cruel practices. He argued against the slavish adherence of Meccans to tradition and custom. In many ways, the teachings of early Islam were a rebellion against the 'asabiyya (loyalties and commitments) of the tribe in Arab society. Muhammad was critical of tribal practices, such as vendettas, and his teachings abrogated collective liability and introduced the institution of individual liability. Muhammad emphasized faith in Allah and submission to His will as the basis for ties and loyalties, rather than the tribe.

The wealthy, powerful members of the Quraysh tribe adamantly opposed Muhammad's message. They instituted harsh persecutions against Muhammad and the early Muslims. Some believers, like Abu Yasir and his wife Umm Yasir, were killed (they are known as the first martyrs of Islam). Others were brutally tortured or savagely attacked. Muhammad himself was regularly mocked and harassed, and he was assaulted at least twice. Despite this persecution, Muhammad gradually won new recruits. His disciples were mainly women, members of the lower classes, and others unhappy with the inequities of Meccan society.

The Quraysh persecution of Muhammad's followers culminated with a boycott of Muslims in Mecca. The Quraysh passed laws prohibiting all business and social relations between Muslims and non-Muslims. The Meccans also implemented a thorough boycott of Muslims, reneged on contracts and deals with Muslims, and took over many Muslim homes and properties. As a result, Muslims living in Mecca could not earn a living; some even starved to death. Meccan leaders also plotted to kill Muhammad and his prominent followers, but the plot failed. Ultimately, this oppression forced the Muslims to begin looking for a new home outside of Mecca.

Because of the Quraysh persecution, Muhammad sent some of his followers to Abyssinia, a land in eastern Africa. A few years later, in the year 622, Muhammad and about 200 followers moved north to the city of Yathrib (later called Medina). This *hijra* ("migration") from Mecca marked a significant turning point in the history of Islam.

Yathrib was a settlement located at an oasis about 200 miles from Mecca. The leaders of Yathrib accepted Muhammad's message, and there Muhammad and his followers founded the first Islamic government. From Medina, Muhammad directed the formation of the Muslim community in other parts of Arabia. The

Muslim population in Medina grew rapidly, and this worried the leaders of Mecca. Over the next few years several battles were fought between the Muslims and Meccans, in which the Muslims held their own.

In 628 Muhammad and his followers decided to travel to Mecca and assert their right to worship at the Kaaba, the ancient sacred shrine, as many other Arabs did. The large number of Muslims who went to Mecca wore the clothing of pilgrims, rather than military garb, and carried only light weapons for hunting and defense, rather than battle gear, in order to emphasize that their intention was not hostile. These Muslims were stopped by a Meccan army, which refused to allow them to continue their pilgrimage. However, the Meccans promised to let the Muslims visit the Kaaba the next year if Muhammad signed a peace agreement. Despite some opposition among his followers, Muhammad agreed to enter a ten-year non-aggression treaty with the Meccans.

In 629, the Muslims made a pilgrimage to Mecca. During this time, the Meccans ordered all of the inhabitants of their city to stay home and lock their doors—according to early Muslim sources, Mecca seemed like a deserted city during their pilgrimage. The Meccan leaders feared contact with the Muslim pilgrims would lead some Meccans to convert.

When the Meccans breached the treaty later in 629, Muhammad raised an army to invade Mecca. By the time Muhammad's forces arrived at the city in January 630, Mecca's inhabitants had lost the will to resist. The city surrendered without a fight, and soon afterward most Meccans converted to Islam and accepted Muhammad as their leader. By the time Muhammad died in 632, he had brought many of the other Arab tribes into the Muslim fold. Soon, most of the people of Arabia lived as followers of Islam.

Islam spread with astonishing speed. As Arab envoys and soldiers fanned out through the region to wage battles and negotiate treaties, the early Muslim community consolidated its power throughout what is now known as the Middle East. Within a hundred years, the

Islamic religious state had conquered the Persian Empire and Islam had spread as far east as the Great Wall of China and as far west as the Atlantic coast of North Africa and the Iberian Peninsula of Europe (the area of modern-day Spain and Portugal). Although Islam was often spread by military conquest of territories controlled by the Byzantine or Persian empires, in many parts of the world the religion spread through peaceful means, such as by missionary work and commerce by Muslim traders.

HISTORICAL BACKGROUND

Muhammad taught his followers that, like Jews and Christians, they were descendents of Abraham, a man who is believed to have lived in the Mesopotamian city of Ur (in present-day Iraq) around 1900 B.C. Abraham followed the commands of God, traveling with

An important moment in Islam's early history occurred in 622 C.E., when Muhammad and about 200 of his followers left Mecca, where they faced persecution. The Muslims settled in Medina, where they soon established the first government based on Islamic principles.

In this painting by Michelangelo, an angel stops Abraham from sacrificing his son to God. Abraham is considered an important patriarch by Jews, Christians, and Muslims.

his family from Ur through modern-day Syria, Lebanon, Israel, and Egypt, where he stopped at Mount Sinai. With his wife Sarah, Abraham bore Isaac, to whom Jews and Christians trace their lineage. Muslims, however, trace their connection to Abraham through his older son Ishmael, whom Abraham conceived with his Egyptian maidservant Hagar. In the Biblical account, Sarah banished Hagar and Ishmael to the desert, where God promised to make Ishmael's descendants a great nation. In Islamic tradition,

Abraham feared that Ishmael would overshadow his younger brother Isaac, so he took Hagar and Ishmael to Mecca and left them there. Islamic tradition also holds that Abraham later returned and he and Ishmael together rebuilt the Kaaba, because the ancient shrine had been damaged in the great flood (the story of which is told in the Biblical book of Genesis).

The connection of Abraham to Islam is very important. Muhammad presented the message of Islam both as a continuation of Judaism and Christianity, and as a departure from these two religions. Muhammad preached a return to the pure message of *islam* (submission to Allah) originally given to Abraham—a message that the Prophet said had been distorted in the development of the Jewish and Christian faiths. Because Muslims believe that the message delivered to the Jews and Christians was divine in origin, they call followers of these religions *ahl al-kitab* ("people of the book"). Also, because followers of these religions were to be protected by the Islamic state, they were referred to as *ahl al-dhimma* ("the protected people"). Muslims also respect the Jewish and Christian scriptures, although they revere the teachings of the Qur'an above all others.

There are other connections between Judaism, Christianity, and Islam. Jerusalem, considered a holy city by both Jews and Christians, is also a holy city to Muslims. During Muhammad's Night Journey, which is described in Sura 17 of the Qur'an, the Prophet traveled from the Kaaba to the Temple Mount in Jerusalem, where al-Masjid al-Aqsa (the Aqsa Mosque) would eventually be built.

The tension between the shared past of these three religions, and Islam's very definite departure from the paths set forth by Judaism and Christianity, has affected relations between the three groups since the founding of Islam.

This Turkish ceramic tile from the 17th century includes the creed, "There is no God but Allah, and Muhammad is His prophet." This statement is the central belief of Islam.

Central Beliefs

Although Islam shares some values with Christianity and Judaism, all its central beliefs are enumerated clearly in the Qur'an, which contains everything Muslims need to know about Allah and His plans for all creation. The teachings of the Qur'an form the foundation of Islamic faith. The most important of these teachings is that Allah is the only god. The Qur'an also establishes guidelines with regard to the moral obligations of the Muslim community.

ALLAH'S FINAL REVELATION

Muslims believe Allah is the all-powerful creator and sustainer of all life, and that he created humans and made all the earth subject to them (Qur'an 22: 65). He alone is worthy of worship, and humans should humbly submit to his will. While Christians believe in a Holy Trinity comprised of the Father, the Son, and the Holy Spirit, Muslims believe Allah does not have children, nor is he surrounded by any lesser gods (Qur'an 23: 91). Muslims are instructed to confess this belief every day. Each time they pray, they declare, "There is no god but Allah."

Muslims believe that Allah controls human history and cares about every individual person, but that He is completely separate from his creation and possesses no human traits. (Although Allah has no gender, Muslims traditionally use the pronouns "He" and "Him" when referring to Allah.) As Qur'an 6: 103 explains, "No vision can grasp Him, but His grasp is over all vision. He is above all comprehension, yet is acquainted with all things." Muslims believe that their holy text does not reveal Allah Himself directly, but merely imparts His will for human beings.

Every human is accountable for all of his or her actions. The Qur'an says that on the Day of Judgment Allah will judge all people on the basis of their individual records, as noted in the book of deeds, and each person will either be admitted into heaven or sent to punishment in hell. Allah is understood by Muslims to be merciful as well as just. He forgives, protects, and rewards those who remain true to His will.

The cosmos as described in the Qur'an resembles that of Christianity and Judaism; it is made up of heaven, earth, and hell. Allah has appointed humans to oversee his creation (Qur'an 2: 30 and 35: 39), but angels, *jinn*, and devils also inhabit the universe. Angels are invisible beings who communicate God's message to the prophets; chief among these is Gabriel, who brought the Qur'an to Muhammad from heaven, and Israfil, who will blow a mighty trumpet to mark the coming of the Day of Judgment. The intelligent beings known as *jinn* (or genies in the West) are also invisible, but like humans they will be judged on the Day of Judgment and sent to either heaven or hell. Any angels and *jinn* who disobey Allah serve Satan, a *jinn* who tempted Adam in the

Garden of Eden. At the time of the final judgment, Satan and his followers will be sent to hell. *Jinn* who do not submit to Allah are known as devils.

Islamic beliefs about sin and human nature are illustrated by the Qur'anic version of events in the Garden of Eden. In the Christian tradition, after Adam and Eve ate the forbidden fruit of the Garden their descendants were doomed to be born with the stain of "original sin," meaning that those descended from Adam and Eve are sinful by nature and require redemption. Christians believe redemption comes only through Jesus Christ, the Son of God, who sacrificed himself on the cross for the sake of humanity. In Judaism, redemption for sins can be found only through adherence to the Law of Moses. By contrast, Islamic tradition does not hold that Adam was cursed by original sin.

A 16th-century painting of Adam and Eve in the Garden of Eden. When the first humans sinned, Allah offered forgiveness and guidance.

Instead, after Adam repented for having eaten fruit from the tree of life, Allah offered forgiveness and declared that He would guide humans when they falter: "And if, as is sure, there comes to you guidance from Me, whosoever follows My guidance, on them shall be no fear, nor shall they grieve" (Qur'an 2: 38). Muslims therefore believe that human beings are not sinful by nature, and that each person is responsible for avoiding or not avoiding sin.

Because Allah is the one true God, His rule extends to all of creation and to all aspects of life, and most Muslims through the centuries have understood Islam to be inseparable from society, law, and government. Human beings, as Allah's agents on earth, have

Jesus, the central figure of the Christian faith, is respected by Muslims. Jesus is considered a messenger whose teachings are universal.

the responsibility of understanding Allah's message and implementing His will.

Muslims believe that Allah designated both prophets and messengers to bear His divine message. The message borne by a prophet is meant for a specific community of people, while that of a messenger is universal. While all messengers are prophets, not all prophets are messengers. The line of messengers began with Noah and includes Abraham, Moses, Jesus, and Muhammad. The Qur'an bestows special status on Jesus—it calls him Messiah, Word, and Spirit—but Muslims do not believe that Jesus was the Son of God, as Christians do. Instead, Islamic belief holds that Muhammad was the greatest and last prophet and messenger. Though Muhammad delivered Allah's universal message, he is often referred to simply as the Prophet.

Allah's message, as dictated to Muhammad, is preserved in the Qur'an. (The name comes from an Arabic word meaning "reading" or "recitation.") Muhammad was merely Allah's instrument for delivering the message. So while Jewish and Christian scholars assert that God revealed Himself through the writers of the scriptures that make up the Torah and the Bible, Muslims believe the Qur'an is the literal word of Allah, with absolutely no input from Muhammad. Muslims also believe that, while the Qur'an continues the message given by Judaism and Christianity, the earlier followers of these two faiths distorted Allah's revelation, thus He needed to send it a final time. The Qur'an is the last revelation from Allah, so no one after Muhammad can claim to be a prophet.

Muhammad received the revelation of the Qur'an over the course of 21 years. During his lifetime it was preserved orally and in written form. The complete text was compiled toward the end of the first half of the seventh century, without any editing or reorganization. Non-Muslims may feel the order of the suras and verses in the Qur'an is random, but Muslims believe the order is divinely inspired. Even today, many Muslims memorize the Qur'an from beginning to end.

THE FIVE PILLARS OF ISLAM

The five essential religious practices required of all Muslims are commonly known as the Five Pillars of Islam. Based on requirements listed in the Qur'an, as well as the practices of Muhammad and the early believers, the pillars are the most visible signs of Muslim faith and the foundation for the unity of all Muslims. The most basic of these is the profession of faith; the others include prayer, the giving of *alms*, fasting, and pilgrimage.

The Islamic profession of faith (*shahada*) goes as follows: "There is no god but Allah and Muhammad is the messenger of Allah." This profession affirms the centerpiece of Islamic theology—the oneness of Allah. This affirmation of one's faith in Allah's oneness is complemented by the recognition of Muhammad as Allah's messenger and as an example for every Muslim.

Muslims offer prayer (*salat*) at different times during each day. The Qur'an mentions three different daily ritual prayers. However, following Muhammad's traditions, Muslims are to perform five daily prayers. When the time for prayer comes, a *mu'adhdhin*, or prayer leader, issues the call to prayer from atop a mosque's minaret. (Today, in some places the call is now an audio recording rather than a live performance). When believers hear the call to prayer, they prepare themselves, then bow in the direction of Mecca to pray. The prayers do not have to be recited immediately: Muslims have a certain amount of time in which to perform each specific prayer after they hear the call.

In many Muslim countries calls to prayer are issued at daybreak, just after noon, at mid-afternoon, at sunset, and in the evening. When Muslims hear the call to prayer, they use small amounts of water to ritually cleanse themselves (and, symbolically, their spirits). They then declare, "Allah is most great," kneel and touch their foreheads on the ground in the direction of Mecca, and recite ritual prayers in Arabic. Muslims also stand, kneel, stand, and prostrate themselves two to four times, depending on the prayer. To conclude their prayers, Muslims recite the profession of faith and repeat the traditional peace greeting twice, saying "Peace be upon all of you and the mercy and blessings of Allah." Each of the five daily prayers lasts between five and ten minutes. It is preferable for believers to pray together when possible; at the very least, Muslim men are expected to recite the noon prayer on Friday at a mosque.

Prayers outside the five daily ritual prayers in Islam are known as the *nafila*, *sunna*, or *mandub* prayers. These prayers are performed exactly like the proscribed prayers, but they are not mandated. Supplications, known as *dua*, include spontaneous praise, pleas, and confession and are often heard at Muslim shrines. Believers perform *dua* by sitting on the floor, holding their hands open, and speaking freely to Allah. Though *dua* are considered informal and personal, many have been collected and recorded in books.

Muslims are obligated to take care of all members of their community and they are expected to help the poor. The third pillar of Islam is *zakat*, or required almsgiving—an annual tax on all Muslims able to pay. This tax—usually 2.5 percent—is on each Muslim's total wealth and assets, not just annual income. Many Muslims use a *zakat* calculator to assess their tax.

Zakat is not the same as charity, because it is obligatory for all Muslims with material goods over and above one's needs. *Zakat* is to be given to the poor, orphans, widows, and travelers, to slaves and debtors, and to help spread the message of Islam, as prescribed in Qur'an 9: 60:

> Alms are for the poor and the needy, and those employed to administer the (funds); for those whose hearts have been (recently) reconciled (to Truth); for those in bondage and in debt; in the cause of Allah; and for the wayfarer.

A secondary form of giving is *sadaqa*, voluntary charity. The most popular time for *sadaqa* is during Ramadan, the ninth month of the Islamic lunar calendar, when Muslims want to make sure everyone has enough to eat during the Feast of the Breaking of the Fast (Eid al-Fitr).

The fourth pillar is fasting (*sawm*) during Ramadan, the month in which Muhammad received his first revelation from Allah in 610 C.E. Ramadan is a time for meditation, prayer, and family gatherings, but the most important aspect of this month is the commandment to fast, which was recorded in Qur'an 2: 183: "O you who believe! Fasting is prescribed to you."

Originally, Muhammad enjoined his followers to follow the tradition of fasting on the Jewish holiday of **Passover**, but after the Battle of Badr in 624, a battle in which Muslims defeated the Meccans, Muhammad declared that Muslims should instead fast during all of Ramadan, and the month-long ritual soon became one of the essential practices of Islam.

Fasting during Ramadan is required of all capable Muslims past puberty. The elderly, the sick, pregnant women, nursing mothers, and travelers do not have to fast during Ramadan, but they must find another time to complete their fast. Those who are terminally ill, or those who cannot make up the missed days of fasting by fasting on other days, are required to pay a certain amount of alms, which excuses them from fasting.

From dawn until sunset, Muslims who are fasting must avoid food, drink, and certain physical activities. The discipline of fasting is designed to help increase Muslims' spiritual focus and symbolizes their purification. While fasting, Muslims thank Allah for his blessings and ask forgiveness for sins. They may also recite the entire Qur'an during Ramadan, reading one-thirtieth of the scriptures each night of the month. Many Muslims attend the mosque for the regular evening prayer, which is followed by a special prayer recited only during Ramadan. After night falls, Muslims break their fast with a light meal; some also share a late evening meal with members of their families.

On the 27th night of Ramadan, Muslims celebrate the night Muhammad began receiving Allah's revelation. The month of Ramadan ends with Eid al-Fitr, the feast of fast-breaking.

Because the Islamic calendar is based on the lunar cycle, the month of Ramadan falls at a different time each year. Fasting during the winter is often less difficult because the days are shorter and the weather not as hot, while fasting during the long, hot days of summer can be very difficult, especially for those who work outdoors.

The fifth pillar of Islam is the requirement that at least once in every adult Muslim's lifetime, he or she is expected to make a ritual pilgrimage (*hajj*) to Mecca if he or she is physically and financially able. The *hajj*, which literally means "to set out for a place," occurs during Dhu al-Hijja, the twelfth month of the Islamic calendar. In any given pilgrimage season, as many as two million Muslims from around the world arrive in Saudi Arabia to make the journey to Mecca. Because the number of pilgrims has grown so large, the Saudi government now regulates the number of pilgrims it will admit from each country, and those who want to make the pilgrimage must apply. For many of those permitted to make the journey, the *hajj* marks a high point of their lives.

The pilgrims' ultimate destination is the shrine known as the Kaaba, an ancient place of worship that is believed by Muslims to have been the site of Allah's covenant with Abraham's son Ishmael. Muhammad cleansed the Kaaba of tribal idols, reclaiming it for Allah and restoring it to its rightful place, according to Qur'an 22: 26–27:

> Behold! We gave the site to Abraham, of the (Sacred) House, (saying), "Associate not anything (in worship) with Me, and sanctify My House for those who compass it round, or stand up, or bow, or prostrate themselves (therein in prayer). And proclaim the Pilgrimage among people."

Some of the *hajj* rituals are rooted in pre-Islamic pilgrimage practices. Among the rituals are walking counter-clockwise around the Kaaba seven times, kissing or touching the black stone located in a wall of the Kaaba, and sacrificing an animal in Mina, ten miles away from Mecca. By including certain tribal practices, Muhammad created a link with the past that helped unite Arab Muslims from various backgrounds into a coherent Islamic community. Pilgrims also reenact Ishmael and his mother Hagar's desperate search for water in the desert, running between Safa and Marwah seven times.

Other rituals symbolize the unity of the global Muslim community. The central ritual of the *hajj* involves praying and meditating

The Kaaba can be seen at the far end of the Great Mosque in Mecca. Each year, approximately 2 million Muslims participate in the pilgrimage to Mecca, one of the five pillars of Islam.

for an entire day on the Plain of Arafat, about 12 miles from Mecca, where Muhammad gave his last message. This is followed by a trip to Mina for the animal sacrifice, where pilgrims first crowd onto Jamarat Bridge and throw pebbles at pillars that represent the devil.

Pilgrims to Mecca symbolize their purification for the journey in their appearance. Men wear sandals and wrap themselves in two pieces of unsewn white cloth; some shave their heads. Women wear a simple version of their normal clothing or a long white dress, with only their hands and faces showing. These plain garments symbolize the equality of all before Allah—during the pilgrimage, no class or cultural differences are to exist.

The *hajj* period ends with a three-day festival called Eid al-Adha, or Feast of Sacrifice. The Eid al-Adha is celebrated by all Muslims around the world at the end of the hajj period, not just by those actually able to make the journey. It is a time of prayer and celebration with family and friends. When pilgrims have completed the *hajj*, many travel north to Medina, where they visit Muhammad's tomb.

THE MUSLIM COMMUNITY

Muslims throughout the world see themselves as a unified community; the ties of faith are stronger than family, tribal, or national bonds. The global community of Muslim believers is known as the **umma**. While only believers belong to the *umma*, any person is welcome to join it. The Qur'an instructs members of the Muslim community to be an example, and to invite others to join their moral society: "You are the best of Peoples, evolved for mankind, enjoining what is right, forbidding what is wrong, and believing in Allah" (Qur'an 3: 110). Muslims are instructed to create a just society, in which people are not exploited and do not suffer. In this kind of society, believers can develop a closer relationship with Allah.

The Qur'an's message about creating a just society challenged

During the feast of Eid al-Adha, it is customary for Muslims to sacrifice a sheep, as this Afghani family is doing. The meat is traditionally divided into three parts, and given to family, relatives, and the poor.

the social order of Muhammad's day. Islam instructs believers to give a portion of their income to the poor and to fast during Ramadan to remind themselves of the poverty of those without adequate food or drink. The Qur'an also commands that believers provide fixed portions of inheritance for women and children, and deal fairly with debtors, widows, orphans, slaves, and the poor. Muslims were also commanded to lay aside their selfishness and express an attitude of humility by prostrating themselves in prayer at proscribed times during each day. These commands became the basis for the subsequent development of Islamic law, which addresses all areas of believers' conduct and to this day provides the guidelines for the daily behavior of Muslims worldwide.

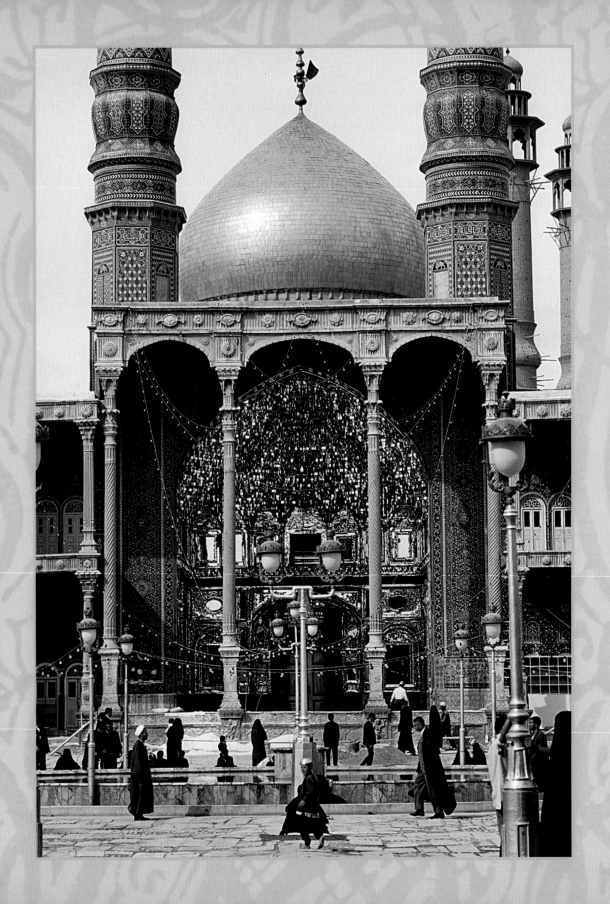

The mirrored entrance to the shrine of Fatima in Qom, Iran. Shiite Muslims consider Qom a sacred city, and more than 400 Shiite saints are buried there.

Islam Divided: The Major and Minor Sects

Within fifty years of the night Muhammad received his first revelation on Mount Hira, Islam had become a codified religion with its own scriptures and rituals, and Islamic belief had spread far beyond the Arabian Peninsula.

But the Muslims had also experienced the first serious split within their ranks—the division into two major religious sects, the Sunnis and the Shiites. This important schism was followed by less radical, but nevertheless significant, separations of smaller communities with varying beliefs, as well as the development of the mystical branch of Islam known as Sufism. Today Islam remains a religion divided.

THE SUNNI-SHIA SPLIT

Sunni Muslims make up more than 80 percent of Islam's adherents worldwide. This main branch of Islam has dominated the religion almost continuously since 661, when the Muslims split into two groups. The smaller of these major groups, the Shiites, make up about 15 percent of Muslims in the world today. Shia Islam is the official religion in Iran, and Shiite Muslims form the largest religious group in Iraq and Bahrain. There are significant numbers of Shiites in Lebanon, Syria, Saudi Arabia, Pakistan, Afghanistan, Azerbaijan, Yemen, and India.

The Sunni-Shia split has come to encompass matters of belief and law, but it developed initially as a disagreement over leadership. When Muhammad died in 632, Muslims had to decide who would lead them and how to choose this leader. This crisis in leadership could have drastically destabilized the young community of believers. When the Muslims met at Thaqifa after the death of the Prophet, Muhammad's closest friends and advisors insisted that a single leader should be chosen to lead the Muslims. The leader would be chosen for his closeness to the prophet, wisdom, piety, and bravery. From 632 to 661, four of Muhammad's most prominent companions served as the Muslim spiritual and political leaders. These leaders were given the title *caliph*, which means "successor."

The first caliph was Abu Bakr, a member of Muhammad's tribe, the Quraysh, and the father of Muhammad's youngest wife Aisha. Abu Bakr had been an early convert to Islam, and was widely respected for his exemplary religious devotion. The tribal unity Islam had fostered on the Arabian Peninsula threatened to deteriorate after Muhammad's death, and Abu Bakr worked to consolidate the support of the Arab tribes before his own death just two years later, in 634.

The next caliph was Umar, also a member of the Quraysh and the father of another of Muhammad's wives. Umar oversaw the first wave of Islamic expansion both east and west. He maintained a large military, and his forces defeated the Persian

Empire as well as Byzantine forces in Syria and Egypt. Many of the people living in the conquered territories converted to Islam; Christians and Jews who decided to remain in their faiths were taxed in exchange for the protection of the Muslim state, but otherwise permitted to continue their own customs and religious practices.

After Umar died in 644, Uthman was selected as the third caliph. Uthman was a member of a prominent Quraysh family from Mecca. He allowed Arabs to take over conquered territories, especially in present-day Iraq, and resentments festered among his soldiers because they felt they received too little pay compared to the newly wealthy Arab landowners. Uthman did advance Islamic

An illustration of the third caliph, Uthman, holding a copy of the Qur'an. Under Uthman's direction, an authoritative text of the Qur'an was compiled.

traditions—under his leadership the first official text of the Qur'an was compiled—but he was not as skillful a political leader as either Abu Bakr or Umar. Rebel troops opposed him, and in 656, he was murdered during one of many rebellions that plagued the young Islamic community.

When Uthman died, Muhammad's cousin Ali became caliph. Ali had been one of Muhammad's earliest converts (he converted as a boy, preceded only by Muhammad's wife Khadija), and he was also Muhammad's son-in-law (he had married Muhammad's daughter, Fatima, by his first wife Khadija). Ali remained a highly influential companion of Muhammad until the Prophet died.

At the time of Muhammad's death, many Muslims expected that Ali would succeed Muhammad. Each time the position of caliph opened, Ali's supporters maintained that he was the rightful leader of the Muslims. His supporters knew Ali as an extremely devout believer who always observed Islamic practices and understood the Qur'an. They believed that Muhammad had named Ali as his successor and consequently that only members of Muhammad's family should be given the position of leader of Islam. These supporters came to be commonly known as the Shiites (from *shiat Ali*, Arabic for "party of Ali").

When Ali finally became caliph, the Muslim community faced civil war. Abu Bakr's daughter Aisha, who had been Muhammad's youngest wife, and Uthman's nephew Muawiya, governor of Syria, both challenged Ali for not doing more to locate and punish Uthman's killers. During the Battle of Siffin (657), Muawiya's soldiers stuck passages from the Qur'an onto the ends of their spears when they felt they were about to lose the battle against Ali. With this, Ali ordered his army to stop fighting. Afterward Ali sought to compromise with Muawiya, a move that offended a group of his own supporters. This group came to be known as the Kharijis ("seceders"), and though Ali's forces defeated them in a decisive battle, one of them murdered Ali in 661.

This Persian fresco shows the martyred Hussein, who was killed at the Battle of Karbala in 680 C.E. The faceless figure holding Hussein represents his father, Ali ibn Abu Talib, the fourth caliph.

Ali's death ended what has come to be known as the era of the "rightly guided caliphs." After Ali's death Muawiya declared himself caliph and inaugurated the Umayyad dynasty, which was to last almost a century. Ali's supporters urged his sons to seek the leadership, but Ali's oldest son Hassan agreed not to pursue his claim to the position of caliph. Hassan died soon after, allegedly poisoned by his enemies. Ali's younger son Hussein also agreed not to vie for the position of caliph until Muawiya died, but while he was still alive Muawiya named his son Yazid his successor as caliph, therefore substituting a hereditary line of rule for the previously established system of electing the most qualified leader. Hussein's followers declared war against Yazid, but they were vastly outnumbered and were defeated at the Battle of Karbala in 680. Hussein and most of his family were killed when he refused to surrender his claim to the caliphate. His infant son Ali survived, however, so the Shiite line of leadership continued.

DIFFERENCES IN THE SHIITE AND SUNNI TRADITIONS

Sunnis and Shiites share the most important beliefs of Islam—the oneness of Allah, adherence to the Qur'an, and the coming of the Day of Judgment. They also agree on the fundamental practices of Islam (the five pillars). The two groups also recognize each other as Muslims. Many Sunnis, however, contend that Shiites put too much emphasis on the stories of their martyrs, primarily Ali and Hussein, at the expense of Muhammad and the origins of Islam. Some also believe that Shiites would rather convert Sunnis to their brand of Islam than cooperate with them.

The name *Sunni* comes from the **Sunna,** the example set by Muhammad (the word *sunna* literally means "the path"). The Sunna are the teachings and practices of the Prophet, as recorded in the **Hadith,** a collection of stories about the words and deeds of Muhammad and the first Muslims. Muslims do not consider the Hadith to be the literal word of Allah, unlike the holy Qur'an, and therefore it does not have the same weight as the Qur'an. However, the stories in the Hadith are used to help Muslims understand their faith and interpret the Qur'an. Both Sunnis and Shiites accept the Hadith; however each group accepts certain stories as canonical while rejecting others.

The rituals of prayer practiced by Sunnis and Shiites differ in some aspects. Although both Sunnis and Shiites recite five prayers each day (*fajr, dhuhr, 'asr, maghrib,* and *'isha'*), Sunnis say their prayers at five different times during the day while Shiites recite the five prayers at three different times of the day. Shiites and Sunnis have the same call to prayer, but Shiites add to the call a reference to the special status of Ali. Both Sunnis and Shiites begin praying in a standing position, then bow, then prostrate themselves, but Sunnis usually prostrate themselves on a prayer rug, if one is available, while Shiites prefer to use a piece of hardened clay (called the *turba*) for this purpose.

The death of Hussein supplied Shia Islam with its central martyr, and his story supplies to this day the most popular Shiite ritual, called the *ta'ziya*. On the tenth day of the month of Muharram (the first

Shiite Muslims in Afghanistan perform a ritual that involves self-flagellation during Ashura, a festival that commemorates the death of Hussein.

month of the Islamic lunar calendar), Shiis commemorate the anniversary of Hussein's death with ritual mourning and reenactments of his martyrdom. The *ta'ziya* involves extensive participation, from weeping to breast beating to **self-flagellation**. This celebration sustains the memory of Hussein's refusal to back away from his beliefs in the face of oppression and death. It also reaffirms the Shiite identity as a community by affirming their direct connection to Muhammad's family, and sets them apart from the Sunni tradition, which traces its connection to Muhammad through the rightly guided caliphs and the body of Islamic law that evolved from their actions and decisions. The reenactment of the tragedy of Hussein's death confirms Shiites' belief that they are an oppressed community, faithful to Allah, working toward a just society and the final victory of justice over oppression at the end of history.

The original differences between Shia Islam and Sunni Islam have broadened through the centuries to include a whole range of spiritual beliefs and practices. But the Shiite belief in leaders descended from the family of Muhammad, which initially tore them away from the Sunnis, still remains. Shiites call their leaders *imams*. These are religious, and sometimes also political, leaders who are thought to be without sin and able to correctly interpret the Qur'an to lead Shiite Muslims in the right direction. Shiites also believe that the imams will intercede on behalf of their followers on the Day of Judgment.

Faithful to the pious examples of Ali and his son Hussein, the early Shiites believed that the Umayyad caliphs were corrupt and had deviated from the path set by Muhammad. They declared that the caliph must be a direct descendent of Muhammad and Ali, whom the Shiites considered the first imam. The Sunnis, in contrast, viewed the caliph as political leaders only (they called their prayer leaders imams). Later, the Sunnis came to put their primary trust in Islamic law and the teachings of religious scholars called the *ulama*.

After the Shiites broke away from the Sunnis, Shia Islam itself became divided, because at different times Shiites could not agree which descendent of Muhammad should lead them. The most decisive split in Shia Islam occurred in the eighth century, when a dispute occurred over who should succeed the sixth imam, Jafar al-Sadiq. The imam had originally selected his oldest son, Ismail, to

Shiite Muslims in Pakistan burn American, British, and Israeli flags in March 2003. Because of their minority status, Shiites have historically considered themselves as representing and defending the oppressed. This protest is in opposition to the U.S. invasion of Iraq.

succeed him, but Ismail died before Jafar al-Sadiq. Jafar then declared his younger son, Musa, as his successor. However, before Ismail died he had named his own son, Mohammad ibn Ismail, as his heir. The Shiites became divided—one group believed that Ismail and his son were the seventh and eighth imams; the other supported Musa as the seventh imam.

This schism resulted in the two major Shia communities, the Twelvers (also known as the Ja'fari Shia), who supported Musa, and the Seveners (also known as Ismailis), who followed the leadership line of Ismail. Twelver Shiites continued to follow Musa and his descendants. A few generations later, in the tenth century, the twelfth imam of Musa's line disappeared mysteriously. Twelver Shiites believe that the twelfth imam will return to earth at the end of time as the *mahdi* to usher in a perfect Islamic society. Sevener Shiites do not believe in a *mahdi* figure and have continued to support an unbroken line of leaders from the family of Ismail.

In the absence of the imam, Twelver Shiites developed a practice in which a council of twelve scholars elects a leader, known as an *ayatollah*, who interprets law and scripture for believers. Twelver Shiism became the state religion in Persia during the 16th century; since that time it has been the largest Shiite sect in Iran. Today, Twelver Shiites also constitute an majority of the Muslims in certain regions of Iraq and Lebanon.

SHIITES AND OPPRESSION

Because of their history, the Shiites consider themselves the voice of the oppressed. They cling to verses like Qur'an 28: 5: "And We wished to be gracious to those who were being depressed in the land, to make them leaders (in faith) and make them heirs." The Twelvers' belief in the *mahdi* is emblematic of this commitment to the downtrodden—they believe that history will culminate with the radical defeat of all injustice. This commitment to justice promotes social activism among Shiites and has also resulted in moving expressions of faith. Shiites believe that simplicity and suffering can wash away the effects of sin and give them the power to defeat their enemies.

The emotional devotion to Shiite traditions is nowhere more evident than in their journeys to the shrines of imams, martyrs, and saints. From its earliest days Shia Islam attracted many poor followers who could not afford to make a pilgrimage to Mecca, so Shiites came to believe that these alternate destinations allowed them to fulfill their pilgrimage obligation and thus find favor with Allah. The most important pilgrimage sites are the tombs of Ali and his son Hussein, which are both located in Iraq. Before the Iran-Iraq War (1980–88), tens of thousands of Shiites from Iran made pilgrimages to these sites every year. Other important pilgrimage sites in Iraq include the tombs of the seventh and ninth imams, which are located near Baghdad. Important Shiite shrines in Iran include the tombs of the eighth imam, Reza, and his sister, Fatima. The tombs are thought to be the dwelling places of the deceased, and pilgrims also approach them to receive spiritual power, seek comfort, and plead for intercession with Allah.

The Shiites also hold in special veneration the Fourteen Pure Ones (or Fourteen Perfect Ones), a group that includes Muhammad, Ali and his wife Fatima, Hussein and his brother Hassan, and the other imams. The members of this group are considered to have been sinless and are models of faith and suffering. As the only woman in this special group, Fatima symbolizes faith, compassion, and sorrow in the face of suffering. Shiites view the intercession of saints on their behalf as an important part of the believer's relationship with Allah.

Sunni Muslims have their own saints and shrines in such countries as Egypt, Turkey, Syria, and India, and praying for the intercession of saints is widespread in both Arab and non-Arab countries with Sunni majorities. A notable exception is Saudi Arabia, where a conservative branch of Sunni Islam, Wahhabism, is dominant. Followers of this form of Islam (who prefer to call themselves *muwahhidun,* or unitarians), disagree with the idea that saints can intercede with Allah on behalf of Muslims.

THE SUFIS

As Sunni Islam developed, the decisions of the *ulama* ensured that *Sharia,* or Islamic law, governed all aspects of Muslim life. However, soon some converts to Islam found the focus on rules and rituals to be stifling and less than spiritually fulfilling. The masses of believers, unlike the scholarly *ulama,* longed for something besides the law to fill their hearts. Without a personality like Muhammad or Ali to model for them a pious life blessed by Allah's presence, some believers turned to **mysticism** as they tried to give meaning to and understand the mysteries of their faith. This movement came to be called Sufism.

Today the word *Sufism* refers to all strains of mysticism within Islam. The word *sufi* is generally translated as "wool" and was taken from the early Sufis' practice of wearing simple woolen garments as a symbol of self-denial.

Technically, Sufism does not constitute another sect within Islam; instead, it is a spiritual practice that follows what Sufis saw as Muhammad's own mysticism, which he exhibited in his solitary retreats and in his closeness to Allah. The Prophet's austerity, modesty, and non-materialism also inspired the Sufi *tariqas* ("orders"), which attempt to imitate Muhammad's humility and way of living. Sufi practices involve **asceticism** and meditation, through which the believer attempts to draw near to Allah in order to experience the divine in a personal way. Sufis believe strongly in Qur'an 50: 16, a verse that says Allah is closer to the human being "than his jugular vein."

Most Sufis hold the same core beliefs as other Muslims, and have the same reverence for the Qur'an. But while codes of conduct based on Islamic law are of the utmost importance to other Muslims, for Sufis, the inner spiritual path—the search for union with Allah—is supreme. All Muslims believe they will draw close

A Persian illustration depicts Muslims performing religious dances. Sufism is a mystical element of Islam that includes the belief that through prayer and meditation, a Muslim can experience direct union with God. Dance, poetry, and music help Sufis reach an ecstatic state that they feel brings their spirits closer to Allah.

to Allah after the Day of Judgment, but Sufis believe that through meditation and self-denial they can experience the closeness of Allah while they are still alive. (The practice of self-denial in order to more correctly perceive God was also widely practiced in early Christianity by such groups as the Gnostics.)

Abu Hamid Muhammad al-Ghazali (1058–1111) was a respected Islamic theologian and member of the *ulama*, who was credited with attempting to re-invigorate Islamic practice and belief. Toward the end of his life, al-Ghazali turned to Sufism as a spiritual method and discipline. He argued that Sufi practices can be reconciled with jurisprudential Islamic practices, but that the law is very important for the attainment of knowledge of Allah. Al-Ghazali's reasoning is significant because he was a highly regarded classical theologian and jurist, so his affirmation of Sufism had a strong impact. His teachings paved the way for Sufism to fit within the parameters of Islamic thought and law. Ghazali emphasized seeking Allah and surrendering to His will not just during ritual prayer and fasting, but also during every-

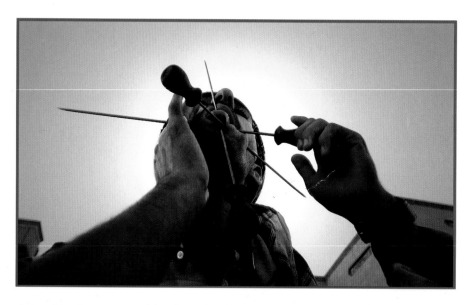

Some Muslim mystics, like this Iraqi Sufi, participate in ceremonies like the *darb*, in which they push skewers through their flesh. To Sufis, this demonstrates that they have acheived union with Allah.

day activities such as eating and sleeping. This teaching provided the foundation for the various Sufi orders that developed after his death.

Sufi leaders, known as *shaykhs* ("masters"), in each order led believers as they are initiated as either *murids* or *dervishes*, different classes of brothers who pledge allegiance to the leader. (It is worth noting that women could join Sufi orders. Some women even played a leading role in Sufism and made a huge impact on later Sufi movements, such as Rabi'a al-'Adawiyya (d. 801), who became a central figure of the spiritual tradition). Many orders spread over wide geographic areas—the first order was based in Baghdad, but later spread to west Africa and southeast Asia—and many established their own monasteries.

Sufis move along the mystical path toward Allah through prayer, fasting, meditation, and the *hal* ("mystical state"), the last of which can never be earned and is only given as a gift from Allah. Sufi orders practice different forms of asceticism, including poverty, silence, and celibacy. Central to Sufi practice is ritual prayer (*dhikr*), in which believers meditate in order to find unity with Allah. This practice, known as "remembering" or "recollecting" Allah, is based on Qur'an 29: 45: "remembrance of Allah is the greatest (thing in life) without doubt." This meditation can be performed silently, but is more often recited loud, and Sufis believe it is impossible to perform it too often. Sufis recite these ritual prayers at any time, either individually or in groups, and they often repeat Allah's name over and over for many hours.

Sufis also use music, song, and dance (*sama*) to enter ecstatic states in which they believe they can experience Allah's presence. Though denounced by the religious authorities, the use of music and dance became very popular in some Sufi orders as a way to rapidly induce a state of ecstasy and awareness of Allah's presence. Sufis gather to sing praises to Allah. The whirling dervishes are the most widely known examples of Sufi dancers. They are members of a Sufi order founded by Jalal al-Din al-Rumi (d.

1273), and their whirling dance is meant to simulate the movement of the universe.

Shiite beliefs influenced Sufism in the early days of both movements. The most important Shiite idea adopted by Sufis is that of the *mahdi*. The Sufis, however, believe the *mahdi* will simply be a divinely guided leader (rather than the returning twelfth imam) who will create a just society at the end of time. Many Muslims in the Sunni tradition now believe in the *mahdi* due to the widespread influence of the Sufis. (A sizeable number of Muslims believe that the coming *mahdi* is Jesus.) Also, the Sufi *shaykhs* are considered spiritual leaders. Some *shaykhs* became so revered that they were believed to have miraculous powers, and their tombs became shrines to which many Sufis made pilgrimages.

Sufism thrived and spread during key periods in Islamic history. When the power of the Sunni caliphate was destroyed by the Mongols in the thirteenth century, Sufism (as well as Shiism) expanded quickly. Soon Sufism was so extensive that it was hard to distinguish from less mystic forms of Islam. As Sufism spread, the Sufis became very effective missionaries of Islam, in part because their fluid traditions allowed them to accept and incorporate non-Islamic practices from the cultures into which they had moved. Sufis have traditionally taken the side of the poor rather than that of the upper classes, which has often made Sufism very attractive to those who feel oppressed.

Most Sufis have attempted to remain apolitical, with some key exceptions. As Western countries like Great Britain and France began colonizing Muslim lands during the eighteenth and nineteenth centuries, some Sufi orders played a large role in resisting *colonialism*. In such places as the Sudan, Sufi orders became politicized and organized rebellions against the foreign invaders. More recently, Sufis have been very active in resisting Russian forces in the province of Chechnya.

Sufi orders have proliferated worldwide in the modern era. They are represented in all schools of thought in Islam and found in all Muslim communities.

OTHER SECTS

Over the centuries, Islam has given rise to more than 70 different sects. Among the most significant outside the Sunnis and Shiites have been the Kharijis, Zaidis, Wahhabis, Nusayris, Druze, and Ahmadiyya. Some of these still exist, but others have died out. Some have developed so many of their own traditions that most Islamic scholars no longer consider them Muslim.

The first division within Islam occurred when the Kharijis left the fold during Ali's rule as caliph (656–661). The Kharijis were followers of Ali who objected when he agreed to negotiate with his chief rival, Muawiya. They removed their support from Ali and thus came to be known as "the ones who leave." They believed that Muslims had strayed from their ordained path, and therefore any Muslims who disagreed with the Kharijis were unbelievers and should be killed. One of their first targets was Ali himself; they assassinated him in 661.

The Kharijis attracted followers in part because Islamic rulers had tended to favor Arabs in general and certain Arab tribes in particular. The marginalized people who joined the Kharijis believed that by following true Islam they could improve their social and economic conditions.

By the eighth century, the Khariji began to moderate their position. The killing of other Muslims was discouraged. The most influential Khariji imam at this time was Abd Allah ibn Ibad. His followers—who became known as Ibadis—founded communities in parts of Africa and southern Arabia; they also became the leaders of Oman, where Ibadi Islam remains the state religion. Today, the Kharijis are gone but Ibadi Muslims remain in Oman, east Africa, the Mzab valley of Algeria, the Nafus mountains of Libya, and the island of Jerba in Tunisia.

After the Sunni-Shia split, another group of Muslims broke away from the Shiites. The Zaidis were followers of one of Ali's great-grandsons, a man named Zaid, who lived in the eighth century. Zaid and his supporters believed that he was the rightful fifth imam, rather than Muhammad al-Baqir. He led a rebellion against the imam, but was killed in 740. Despite his death, Zaid's followers accepted him as the true imam, and continued to support his descendants.

Although Zaidi Islam is consider an offshoot of Shia Islam, in their theology and law Zaidis are actually closer to Sunnis than to other Shiites. The Zaidis do not place the same importance on the imam, and disagree with the Shia belief in the *mahdi*, for example. Most Zaidis live today in Yemen, which until the 1960s was ruled by a Zaidi caliph.

Another sect, al-Nusayris, consider themselves Muslims, but most Muslims do not see them as part of Islam. Under the leadership of a man named Muhammad ibn Nusayr, they broke away from other Shiites in the ninth century. The Nusayris worship Ali, Muhammad, and the early Shiite saint Salman as a divine trinity. They also reject the Qur'an, keep most of their prayers and beliefs secret, believe in reincarnation for men (women are thought not to have souls at all), and incorporate some elements of Christianity into their beliefs. They do not have public places of worship and do not follow Islamic law. Today the Nusayris number over a million; most live in Syria.

The Nusayris never managed to gain acceptance within mainstream Islam. Nusayrism was treated as heretical movement and was often persecuted. In recent years, the Nusayris have tried to change perceptions of their sect by calling themselves 'Alawis—a historical term for Shia Islam. The former Syrian president Hafez al-Asad, a Nusayri who was aware of the sect's highly problematic position in Islamic history, was one of the first to refer to his sect as the 'Alawis. In doing so, Asad gave the impression that he belonged to a more mainstream Shiite branch of Islam. There is no evidence, however, that the Nusayris have altered their long-held theological positions, so as to become doctrinally closer to Shiism.

The Druze, an offshoot of the Sevener Shiites (Ismailis), emerged in the eleventh century when a Sevener leader named al-Hakim (d. 1021) asserted that he was the divine link between Allah and

Imam Shah Zaid battles his enemies in this 17th-century Persian fresco. Today, Zaidi Islam is a small sect, and most Zaidis live in Yemen.

humans. Al-Hakim later disappeared, and his followers believe he will return to earth to institute justice. Many Muslims do not consider the Druze to be true followers of Islam, because the Druze have their own holy scriptures and laws. They keep their beliefs and practices secret in order to avoid persecution by people outside their faith. There are two classes of Druze: the *juhhal*, or ignorant ones, who are not completely initiated into the faith, and the *uqqal*, or initiated, who are wise and lead exemplary lives.

The Druze have a tightly knit community; they do not accept converts and they do not marry outside the faith. They number in

A group of Druze religious leaders in the Galilee. Most members of this secretive sect live in Israel, Lebanon, or Syria.

the hundreds of thousands today, mainly in Syria, Israel, and Lebanon.

In the eighteenth century, a man named Muhammad ibn Abd al-Wahhab (d. 1792) advocated a return to the original purity of Islam. He asserted that every new idea or practice adopted by Muslims after the tenth century was contrary to the truth of Islam and must be eradicated. He called for a literal understanding of the Qur'an as the basis for Islamic law, and he rejected both mysticism and the worship of beloved Islamic leaders as saints.

With support from the powerful Al Saud family, al-Wahhab's beliefs spread throughout the Arabian Peninsula. Today, most of the people of Saudi Arabia adhere to Wahhabism (There are some Shiites, especially in the eastern part of the kingdom). It is an extreme brand of the faith—Wahhabis feel that theirs is the only true path of Islam, and do not accept other Muslim groups or sects as legitimate.

In 1889, a man named Ghulam Ahmad (d. 1908) who lived in India founded the offshoot of Islam known as Ahmadiyya. He declared himself the *mahdi* and accepted support from the British colonial rulers of India, who at the time had a political stake in developing an alternative to Sunni Islam. The Ahmadiyya's belief in Ahmad's divine status sets them apart from Sunni Muslims, but they do subscribe to the central Sunni interpretations of Islamic law and they have adopted most Sunni practices. Ahmadiyya is now split into two branches: the Lahore, which Sunnis recognize as Muslim, and a larger group, the Qadiyanis, which other Muslims do not recognize as legitimate.

The Ahmadiyya exhibit great missionary zeal and have spread through much of the world, particularly in the West. Their total number is estimated to be as high as 10 million.

Law and Practice

Codes of conduct occupy a central place in Islamic life because Muslims believe that each person will face Allah on the Day of Judgment and be held accountable for his or her actions. As a result, the law (*Sharia*) is supreme in Islam. But although the Qur'an contains specific laws pertaining to marriage, divorce, inheritance, contracts, governmental affairs, torts, and some criminal laws, it is not a book of laws. A fully authoritative body of Islamic law took shape over several hundred years.

The word for Islamic law, *Sharia,* literally means "path to water." *Sharia* is believed to be a complete guide for every aspect of Muslim life. *Sharia* treats five different kinds of behavior: obligatory, recommended, permissible, reprehensible, and forbidden. Both obligatory and forbidden acts carry consequences with or without action: performing an obligatory act is rewarded and failing to perform it is punished, while performing a forbidden act is punished and refusing to perform it is rewarded. The early jurists studied every specific kind of human behavior and prescribed exactly how obligatory and recommended acts should be performed. Every command and every prohibition is supported by an identifiable text in either the Qur'an or the Hadith. However, it is also possible to identify in Islamic law traces of many non-Muslim legal systems, such as Arab tribal law, Roman law, Jewish law, and legal codes from many of the lands conquered by Islamic forces.

THE SOURCES OF ISLAMIC LAW

Sunni Muslim jurists and legal scholars relied heavily on local customs as they began to interpret the Qur'an and establish codes of conduct, and jurists in different locales developed contradictory laws based on different customs. These differences are best illustrated in the approaches of two different scholars of the Umayyad period, one of them in Medina and the other in the newer, more urban city of Kufa. In Medina, Malik ibn Anas depended on the Qur'an, the example of Muhammad, and Arab traditions. He also relied heavily on precedents set by the Prophet's companions in Mecca and Medina. In cases where the language of the Qur'an was ambiguous, Malik considered the practice and customs of the Prophet's companions to be determinative. By contrast, in Kufa Abu Hanifa al-Numan blended Arab and non-Arab traditions in creating the law.

After the Abbasid caliphate replaced the Umayyad in 750, a new group of Sunni jurists, the *ulama*, was created to discern Allah's will and codify the law. The *ulama* determined that there were four sources of law: the Qur'an; the exemplary behavior of Muhammad (the Sunna) as recounted in the Hadith; reasoning by *analogy*; and the consensus of the community.

The primary source of Allah's revelation and law is the Qur'an. Though it includes only a limited number of specific legal rules, the Qur'an does offer broad moral guidelines and provides Islam with its core values.

The second source of law is the Sunna, or stories recorded in the Hadith. The Sunna recounts Muhammad's behavior and the behavior he permitted among his closest companions and the early Muslim community. After Muhammad's death, Muslim scholars faced the challenge of determining which of the many thousands of words and actions attributed to the Prophet and his companions were authentic. Some of them, after all, were fabricated tales offered by people who simply wanted to legitimize their own practices. The *ulama* gradually developed ways to weed out the inauthentic reports, and by the tenth century six collections of Sunna were finally blessed as authentic. Two of these six sources were considered the most authoritative and remain the most important.

The third source of law, reasoning by analogy, was designed to limit personal judgment in rulings. When faced with new problems, jurists looked for a similar or analogous situation in the Qur'an and Hadith. This provided a way to maintain the focus on the Qur'an and the Hadith during the days of Islam's rapid expansion across many cultures. No matter the cultural situation, jurists could identify a similar situation in one of Islam's central texts.

Consensus of the community was the fourth source of law. Two kinds of consensus played a role. Consensus of the entire Muslim community was needed for the religious duties practiced by all Muslims, and the consensus of the *ulama* jurists was needed when different jurists offered different opinions. These opinions were then considered by other jurists and over the years were either accepted or rejected.

Historically, in the Muslim world a single system of courts implemented both *Sharia* and state regulatory laws. Today, in many Muslim countries *Sharia* courts are confined to matters of family law, while *secular* courts deal with criminal and commercial matters.

Sunni Muslims have traditionally followed one of four schools of law, each of which is named for a scholar of the ninth to eleventh centuries who lived in a different geographic region. These schools of law are the Shafii, the Maliki, the Hanafi, and the Hanbali. Each school developed laws in four areas—rituals, contracts, marriage and family, and penal codes. Jurists in these schools often differed in their interpretation of the *Sharia*, but all the interpretations are recognized by Sunni Muslims as legitimate.

Over the centuries there have been a large number of Sunni schools of law that have become extinct. Some of these schools survived for many centuries, before becoming extinct in the modern age. A few, such as the Zahiriyya, Jaririyya, Thawriyya, and al-Awza'iyya, continue to influence the thought of contemporary Muslims and of reform movements.

Shia law differs from the Sunni tradition in several ways. For Twelver Shiites, the sayings of Muhammad's cousin Ali, Ali's wife Fatima, and the other eleven imams are as important and authoritative as the Sunna of Muhammad and his companions. Shiites also look to an organized clergy for guidance in the law, while the Sunnis do not. Also, while Sunnis follow a more strictly literal interpretation of the Qur'an, Shiites allow for more latitude in interpretation and give their imams significant power to make legal rulings. Shia leaders thus have a greater role in interpreting the Qur'an, and therefore exert a greater influence over Shiite society.

FAMILY LAW

Through the centuries the family has remained the basic unit of Muslim life, and family law occupies a central place in Islamic law. The law details the rights and responsibilities of family members in all domestic matters, including marriage, divorce, the custody and care of children, inheritance, and property. Though much of Islamic family law has remained intact, it has been modified in some regions because of increasing cultural pressures. The question of women's rights in particular has inspired movements to reform the law.

The Arab societies of Muhammad's time were *patriarchal*. Men were the leaders of families and tribes. Women had very few rights—they could not inherit money or property, and widows were considered the property of their deceased husband's family. *Polygyny*, or the practice of having multiple wives, was widespread, and men could marry or divorce at will. Boy children were more highly prized than girl children. Some poor families buried their girl children alive because they lacked the financial means to feed and raise them.

One accomplishment of Islam was to create a unity of believers that transcended tribal affiliations. The revelation given to Muhammad also improved the status of women. Qur'an 4: 3 amended the existing custom that allowed men to take unlimited wives; Muslims were permitted four wives, but only if the man could afford to care for each of them equally. In the modern era, some Muslims have proposed that another verse in the Qur'an (4: 129) supports *monogamy*. This verse reads, "You can never be equitable in dealing with more than one wife, no matter how hard you try. Therefore, do not be so biased as to leave one of them hanging (neither enjoying marriage, nor left to marry someone else). If you correct this situation and maintain righteousness, God is Forgiver, Most Merciful." Today, some Muslim countries have limited the practice of polygyny.

Marriage is a sacred contract that protects against sexual misconduct and perpetuates the family as the basic unit of society. All Muslims are expected to marry unless they are either financially or physically unable. The only specification for marriage is an offer and acceptance on the part of two qualified parties in the presence of two witnesses; no religious ceremonies are required. In most places, marriage has traditionally been more of a contract between two families than the union of two individuals. Women cannot, however, be forced into marriage against their wishes, and a woman may stipulate that her husband cannot take another wife, or may reserve the right to divorce him should he choose to do so. While a Muslim man can marry a non-Muslim woman, as long as that person is Jewish or Christian, a Muslim woman cannot marry a non-Muslim man unless the man converts to Islam.

Upon marriage, a woman receives a **dowry** from her husband (in pre-Islamic Arabia, this was paid to the bride's father instead). This becomes her personal property, over which her husband has no legal right. Traditionally, in return for her husband's financial support a wife obeys her husband, takes care of their home, and oversees the education and moral training of their children.

Divorce (*talaq*) is not taken lightly in Islamic law. In pre-Islamic Arabia men could divorce their wives at will, but in Islamic law a husband must divorce his wife three times to make it irrevocable. Qur'an 4: 35 first counsels arbitration when divorce is discussed. If this fails, the advisable course is for the husband to say "I divorce you" once and enter a three-month waiting period to see if the couple can reconcile and to make sure the wife is not pregnant. If the husband reconsiders, the couple can get back together. If they do not reconcile, and the husband utters the divorce declaration twice more, their divorce is final. In another approach, the husband makes the declaration of divorce once each month for three months. At any time during this three-month period, the couple can stop the divorce action, but at the end the divorce is irrevocable. The most frowned upon, and yet most common, type of divorce is the triple *talaq*, in which the husband utters the divorce formula three times all at once.

Women can sue for divorce only on limited grounds, such as the impotence or insanity of her husband or for desertion or failure to support. Quite often, however, women do not exercise their right to divorce because, in many male-dominated societies, they are not informed about their legal rights. In recent years some Muslim countries have expanded their laws to give women more grounds for divorce and to provide women with more material compensation when their husbands divorce them.

In recent years, the practice of stipulated divorces (known as *talaq al-tafwid*) has become more popular. The Prophet Muhammad sanctioned this practice during the early years of

In 2003, the government of Malaysia overruled a controversial decision by an Islamic cleric that permitted the *talaq*, or declaration of divorce, to be sent by text message over a mobile phone. In Malaysia, and other countries with *Sharia* courts, the divorce declaration is supposed to be uttered in front of a court judge.

Islam, but there was much culture-based resistance. In these cases, a stipulation is entered into the marital contract dictating that if the husband commits certain conduct, the wife acquires an immediate right to a divorce. In effect, the stipulation acts as a prenuptial agreement that grants women considerable power within a marriage by challenging the traditionally exclusive male prerogative over divorce. In the modern age, a large number of women rekindled this practice by entering into prenuptial agreements granting wives the right to divorce their husbands.

When divorce occurs, children enter the custody of either the mother or the father depending on their age. In most instances, boys under the age of nine and girls under the age of 12 are given into the custody of the mother. Thereafter, custody reverts to the father.

In Muhammad's day, inheritance was passed only to men; the

nearest male relative of the deceased received the inheritance, even if a female relative was more closely related. Qur'an 4: 11–12 granted women the right to inherit property. Qur'an 4: 7–11 stipulates that wives, daughters, sisters, and mothers of the deceased are entitled to their share of the inheritance before the remainder is passed on the nearest male relative. In most cases, men were given twice the inheritance of women, the reasoning being that they were expected to bear financial responsibility for every member of the their households.

LEGAL GUIDELINES FOR DAILY LIVING

Aside from family law, two other areas of law, pertaining to personal cleanliness and diet, have a great effect on individual Muslims' day-to-day lives.

A student waits to be called on at an elementary school in Baghdad that is operated by Shiite clerics. Girls and boys attend the school on alternate days of the week, because Shiites believe they should be educated separately.

Ritual *ablutions* are required of Muslims to create purity of heart before each of the daily prayers. Following a specific commandment in Qur'an 5:6, the believer pronounces Allah's name before washing his or her hands, forearms, face, head, mouth, nose, ears, and feet. The Qur'an also makes clear that Muslims should strive for cleanliness in all other aspects of life as well: "For Allah loves those who turn to Him constantly and He loves those who keep themselves pure and clean" (Qur'an 2: 222). The Qur'an offers few specific instructions for personal hygiene (Qur'an 74: 4 says believers should keep their clothes clean), but based on teachings in the Sunna, Muslims are expected to perform many kinds of personal cleansing. Among these are regular baths, baths before festivals, ritual baths after sex and menstruation, baths after burying the dead, removal of body hair, regular brushing of the teeth, and keeping streets and public areas clean and tidy.

Islamic law also stresses bodily health as essential to purity of heart and a sound intellect. To this end, Islamic law calls for eating in moderation and discourages overindulgence. The Hadith also prohibits certain foods, including alcohol, pork, blood, and the flesh of animals that have not been slaughtered according to an Islamic ritual that asks for Allah's blessing. Therefore, many Muslims will refuse meat when they are not sure how it was slaughtered. Other Muslims, particularly in the West, do eat commercially prepared meat (other than pork) and say a blessing over it before eating. Meat that meets the Islamic legal requirements is referred to as *halal*.

A Muslim prays in front of the Eid Gah Mosque in Kabul, Afghanistan, on the first day of Ramadan. Muslims observe Ramadan, the ninth month of the Islamic lunar calendar, as a time of fasting and self-sacrifice.

Islamic Celebrations

Muslims celebrate annual religious holidays. Though some customs may vary, the purpose of the celebrations is the same from one country to the next.

According to the Western calendar, the dates of most Islamic celebrations vary from year to year. This is because the Islamic calendar is based on the cycles of the moon. Both the Islamic and Western calendars have twelve months. However, in the Islamic calendar the length of months is based on the intervals between new moons, so months alternate between 29 and 30 days in length. A lunar year has either 355 or 354 days, so it is 10 or 11 days shorter than the solar year.

A new month traditionally begins with the first

sighting of the new crescent moon. (For centuries Muslims have been mathematically calculating the beginning of each month and creating their calendars on the basis of these calculations.) The twelve months of the Islamic calendar are Muharram, Safar, Rabia Awwal, Rabia Thani, Jumada Awwal, Jumada Thani, Rajab, Shaban, Ramadan, Shawwal, Dhu al-Qida, and Dhu al-Hijja.

The Islamic calendar began with the *hijra*, the migration of Muhammad and his followers from Mecca to Medina. According to the Western calendar, the *hijra* occurred on July 16, 622; in the Islamic calendar, this migration is said to have occurred on the first day of Muharram in the year 1 A.H. (A.H. is an abbreviation for the Latin phrase *Anno Hegirae*, meaning "year of the *hijra*").

MAJOR CELEBRATIONS

The major holidays on the Islamic calendar have their roots in the Qur'an or in the teachings of Muhammad as recorded in the Hadith. Fridays are set aside for congregational prayers, while important religious holidays include the observance of Ramadan, Laylat al-Qadr, Eid al-Fitr, and Eid al-Adha.

Every Friday, Muslims gather together at the local mosque for the daily noon prayer. This is known as *Yawm al-Jumua* (literally, "the day of congregation"). Muslim men are required to attend this prayer, but there is a disagreement in Islamic law on whether women are obligated to attend. The Wahhabis maintain that it is preferable that women not attend Friday prayers, but other Islamic schools of thought maintain that it is either obligatory or recommended that women attend Friday prayers.

If women do attend the prayer service, they are often separated from the men. This could be a physical separation, such as behind a curtain or in a side room, or a symbolic one, in which the women form prayer lines behind the prayer lines of men. Muslims at Friday prayers line up side by side. First, the believers listen as the mosque leader (the imam) preaches a short message based on a verse from the Qur'an. Then, the mosque leader directs the Muslims in prayer while facing a niche (*mihrab*) that points in the direction of Mecca. This service usually begins at noon and lasts less than an hour. Afterward, people visit with each other at the mosque.

After attending the service, Muslims may return to their work or they may rest or visit with family and friends for the remainder of the day. However, in some countries, Muslims take off work either Thursday or Saturday plus Friday for a two-day break. In the United States, where many businesses and offices are open Monday through Friday and workers are off on Saturday and Sunday, Muslims normally take a couple of hours from their jobs or businesses to go to the Friday service at the local mosque. Occasionally, in workplaces where a large number of Muslims are employed, a room in the workplace may be prepared for Friday prayers so the workers can conduct the service themselves.

Ramadan, the ninth month of the Islamic calendar, is the month of obligatory fasting. On the first morning of Ramadan, Muslims get up before sunrise to eat a pre-dawn light meal called *Suhur*. This recommended meal provides nourishment for the period between dawn and sunset, when Muslims must not eat, drink, or engage in a variety of physical activities. The daily fast ends after sunset, when Muslims take the evening meal known as the *Iftar*.

During the day, devout Muslims spend as much time as possible in prayer, either privately at home or with others at the mosque. They then gather for Ramadan events in the evening, such as recitation of the nightly Ramadan prayer (*tarawih*), readings of the Qur'an, and Sufi chantings. Believers then sleep, waking before dawn to take another light meal, and the process begins again. The Ramadan observance lasts for the entire month.

Voluntary charity (*sadaqa*) for the poor and needy is very important during Ramadan. This often consists of gifts of money or goods to individuals or charitable organizations and ensures that all have enough to eat during the festival at the end of Ramadan.

In most Muslim countries, Ramadan is a very festive time for believers. Cities festoon the streets with lights and flowers, and local businesses decorate their shops. Muslims greet each other with the saying *Ramadan Mubarak*, which means "a blessed Ramadan." In general, Muslims do not give up their daytime routines, including work, though fasting is considered in part an act of self-discipline by which believers can retreat from everyday life to draw closer to Allah.

While customs associated with Ramadan do vary from country to country, numerous similarities also exist. In many places, candy is distributed to children after the *tarawih* prayer. Certain foods are considered special treats during Ramadan—dates, for example, are widely eaten to break the daily fast, since Muslims believe that Muhammad was fond of dates and often ended his own fasts by eating them. Special foods are also prepared for Ramadan. In India, for example, a special soup thought to quench thirst and produce energy is served in mosques for the daily breaking of the fast. In some countries, special religious programs are shown on television during Ramadan. Also, most Muslims wear new clothes during Ramadan as a way to symbolize their purification during the season.

The 27th day of Ramadan commemorates the sacred night Laylat al-Qadr ("the Night of Power"). On this night, Muslims remember the first revelation Muhammad received from Allah. According to Qur'an 97: 3–4, on the Night of Power the angels descend to earth at Allah's bidding. Muslims consider this a good time to ask for Allah's blessings, and devout Muslims often pray throughout the entire evening. They may also stay awake reading and studying the Qur'an.

Muhammad did not specify the exact night to be celebrated as the Night of Power, though 27 Ramadan has become the traditional date. Muhammad did suggest that Laylat al-Qadr should fall in the last 10 days of the month, so some Muslims take this entire period off from work and seclude themselves for intense prayer and study of the Qur'an.

The end of Ramadan is marked by the festival of fast-breaking,

A Palestinian boy recites Arabic prayers as women relatives pray over the grave of a family member. Muslims visit the graves of loved ones after morning prayers at the end of Ramadan, on the first day of the Eid al-Fitr feast.

known as Eid al-Fitr. This festival begins on the first day of Shawwal, the tenth month of the Islamic calendar. On 29 Ramadan, Muslims watch the western horizon for the crescent moon just after sunset; if they do not see the moon, they fast for another day before beginning the festival. In many Muslim countries, Eid al-Fitr is a national holiday, and business and government offices usually close for part or all of the celebration. Though Eid al-Fitr is considered the lesser of the two major Muslim celebrations (the other is Eid al-Adha, which occurs at the end of the *hajj*), it is more widely publicized and better known in the West.

Shiite Muslims in West Beirut, Lebanon, celebrate Ashura with a mock battle.

The Eid al-Fitr festival lasts for three days, during which family members come together to socialize, exchange gifts, and dine on special foods, many of them prepared only for this annual event. Many people wear new clothes and decorate their homes. On the first morning of the festival, Muslims gather in the local mosque to recite a special prayer, called *Salat al-Id*, and hear a sermon. Other services may be held at the mosque and processions of believers wind through the streets. The highlight of the day is a celebratory meal known as *Id Kah*—the first meal Muslims eat during the day after Ramadan. Family and friends gather for this feast, and children are often given gifts and sweets. All Muslims who can afford to give to the poor and needy are expected to do so, just as they are expected to be generous during Ramadan.

Another important festival occurs at the end of the pilgrimage season; it is known as Eid al-Adha, the festival of sacrifice. Emphasizing commitment, obedience, and self-sacrifice, the festival commemorates Abraham's willingness to obey Allah by sacrificing his son Ishmael. According to Muslim traditions, Allah told Abraham to take his son Ishmael into the mountains and prepare him to be sacrificed. Abraham did this as Allah commanded. He built an altar, tied his young son's hands, and raised his knife to sacrifice Ishmael to Allah. Before Abraham could bring the knife down, Allah ordered him to stop, free his son, and sacrifice a ram instead.

The festival begins on the tenth day of Dhu al-Hijja, the last month of the year, and in most places it lasts for several days. On the first day of the festival, Muslims put on their best clothing and go to the local mosque for a special prayer and a short sermon. Afterward, people visit at the mosque or socialize in the homes of family and friends, where they eat large meals of dishes prepared especially for the feast. Children are often given gifts and sweets. The traditional greeting is *Eid Mubarak*, which means "holiday blessings."

Also important to Eid al-Adha is the sacrifice of animals to commemorate Abraham's sacrifice. This sacrifice is similar to the sacrifice ritual performed by believers who visit Mecca during the *hajj*. Muslims who can afford to purchase an animal for sacrifice (often a sheep) will have them slaughtered, often in a public place. The meat is traditionally distributed in three parts—one part for the poor, one part as a gift to friends and extended family, and one part for the immediate family. Muslim families that cannot afford the expense of sacrificing a sheep may simply purchase meat to eat and give away.

OTHER CELEBRATIONS

In addition to these major festivals, many Muslims commemorate important events in the history of Islam. These include Mawlid al-Nabi, Laylat al-Isra' and al-Miraj, Laylat al-tawbah, Ashura, and Al-Hijra. Though these celebrations are very popular in many parts of the world, they are not mentioned in the Qur'an or Hadith, so some Muslims consider them recent innovations that should not count as religious holidays.

Though no verifiable record exists of the exact date of Muhammad's birth, Muslims around the world celebrate the Prophet's birthday on 12 Rabia Awwal in the celebration commonly known as Mawlid al-Nabi ("birth of the Prophet"). This celebration probably took hold in Egypt in the tenth century, when believers began special chants and festivities to mark Muhammad's birth, and it has become the most popular innovative celebration in Islam. It is a major holiday in some countries, including Egypt and Turkey, but because the early Muslim community did not celebrate it, other countries (chief among them Saudi Arabia) do not recognize or celebrate it at all.

No special prayers or religious services are conducted on this day, but Muslims express their love for Muhammad by gathering to listen to speeches and poems celebrating the Prophet's life and example. In other places, Muslims may also set off fireworks to announce the day, wear new clothes, gather with friends and family, and exchange gifts.

Many Muslims also celebrate Laylat al-Isra' and al-Miraj, the night of Muhammad's miraculous Night Journey from Mecca to Jerusalem and his ascension into heaven. The story goes that two archangels visited Muhammad while he slept and filled his heart with wisdom and faith. Then, in the course of a night, Muhammad traveled from Mecca to Jerusalem and back on a winged creature called al-Buraq. From Jerusalem he ascended into heaven, where he visited with Allah and earlier prophets. During his time in heaven, Muhammad was told that it would be the duty of Muslims to pray five times a day.

The story is mentioned briefly in Qur'an 17:1 and expounded on at some length in the Hadith. Though the Qur'an mentions no specific day for this event and no record exists that Muhammad and the early community celebrated this night, Muslims have set the date as 27 Rajab. Many mark it with special gatherings in homes and mosques, where the story of

A 16th-century Persian illustration shows Muhammad riding the winged
steed al-Buraq during the Prophet's "Night Journey."

Muhammad's Night Journey is told through poetry, chants, and sermons.

Laylat al-tawba (or laylat al-Ghufran) is the "night of repentance" and is observed on 15 Shaban, the month before Ramadan. Muslims who celebrate it believe that all who ask Allah for forgiveness on this night will receive it. It is also considered a night of preparation for Ramadan.

The celebration of Ashura, on 10 Muharram, is especially important to Shiites. On this day, they mark the martyrdom of Muhammad's grandson (and Ali's son) Hussein in Karbala by publicly reenacting the events surrounding his death and participating in elaborate mourning rituals, including chest-beating and weeping.

Muslims from the Kashmir province of India visit Hazratbal, a shrine where a revered relic is kept. Each year many Muslims make pilgrimages to holy sites or the shrines of saints or martyrs.

The 10th day of Muharram has been a significant day to Muslims since the beginnings of Islam. The day is believed to be the anniversary of a number of other occasions significant in history, including the day Noah left the ark after the Great Flood and the day on which Muslims were told to pray in the direction of Mecca, rather than Jerusalem.

Al-Hijra is the first day of the Islamic year. Though this day is not celebrated in any elaborate way, it remains important to Muslims because it is the anniversary of Muhammad's journey from Mecca to Medina (the *hijra*) and was chosen by the second caliph, Umar, to mark the beginning of the Islamic calendar.

Some Sunni Muslims also celebrate the birth and death days of revered figures in Islam, while most Shiites still follow the tradition of visiting the shrines of their imams.

A group of American Muslims pray in a park in New York City. Muslims have become the third-largest religious group in the United States; an estimated 6 million Americans follow Islam.

Issues in Contemporary Islam

Islam is the world's second-largest religion, and Islamic teachings shape the everyday lives of Muslims around the globe. But those who practice traditional Islamic values sometimes find themselves at odds with the norms of modern societies, particularly the popular culture and political systems of the West. The differences between Islam and these outside influences has led to disagreement among Muslims about how to preserve Islam for an uncertain future.

The urge to reform is almost as old as Islam itself. Only five decades into the history of Islam, after Muslims had begun spreading their traditions and in turn incorporating the practices of the societies they conquered, the Kharijis broke away from the larger group of believers, arguing that Islamic traditions and beliefs were being weakened and that Muslims should return to the roots of their faith. But while the Kharijis were among the first Muslims to push for purification of the religion, they certainly would not be the last.

One contemporary reform movement in Islam is often described as fundamentalist. The word *fundamentalism* refers to an effort to purify a religion by establishing and abiding by the fundamental beliefs of that religion. Fundamentalist movements have taken hold in every major world religion, including Islam. Islamic fundamentalists believe that Islam is under attack by corrupt outside values, and they blame both Muslims, for straying from the straight path of Islam, and secular influences for trying to destroy their faith. Islamic fundamentalists (also known as Islamists) want to purify Islam of all corrupting influences. Islamists believe Islam is a comprehensive system of religion, government, and social values, and they support the idea of national governments rooted in Islamic law. In recent years Islamist movements have had enormous effects throughout the Muslim world.

Another reform movement is known as modernist. Modernists are Muslims who attempt to combine Islamic beliefs with the best ideas of the West to meet the challenges of living in the modern global society. Historically, a challenge of modernism has been confronting such issues as the development of the nation-state, democratic governments, and the role of religion in the modern state. Modernists are also challenged by the universal values represented by international law and human rights.

Both modernism and fundamentalism in Islam are responses to pressures on Islam in the modern world—pressures from outside to accept secular views of the relationship between society, government, and religion, and pressures from within to preserve centuries-old traditions in the face of contemporary realities. Modernism seeks to accommodate new ideas within Islam, while Islamism seeks stricter adherence to the vision of Islam set forth in the Qur'an and Hadith.

ISLAM INTO THE MODERN PERIOD

The Abbasid caliphs ruled over the high period of the Arab Islamic empire during the eighth, ninth, and tenth centuries. However, after this the Abbasids' vast empire began to break apart. As smaller Islamic states began to emerge, Muslims in the Arab world were forced to battle invading Europeans in a series of religious wars called the Crusades during the eleventh and twelfth centuries. The Abbasid empire was ultimately destroyed by the Mongols, fierce warriors from Asia, who invaded the region during the thirteenth century. But Islam remained the dominant religion—the Mongols themselves converted by 1313—and new Islamic empires soon arose. From Turkey, the powerful Ottoman empire emerged. In 1453 the Ottomans captured Constantinople, ending the thousand-year rule of the Byzantine empire, and by the 17th century the Ottoman sultans controlled large parts of the Arabian Peninsula, North Africa, Central Asia, and Eastern Europe. In the area of present-day India and Pakistan, the Moghul empire came to power in the 16th century, while at the same time the Shiite Safavid empire ruled Persia.

By the 18th century, however, these Islamic empires were also in decline. They were plagued by internal dissension, as well as by the increasing military power of European countries, which restricted Islamic expansion. European powers like Great Britain, Russia, Austria, and France captured territories from the Ottoman and Moghul empires. Reforms and active resistance by Islamic organizations were not enough to keep the Europeans at bay. By the start of the 20th century, much of the Muslim world was under some measure of European control.

As Islamic societies clashed with Europeans and other cultures during this period, various fundamentalist movements took hold. In Africa, for example, a series of "holy wars" (*jihads*) were declared to make Islamic principles the basis of government. These movements developed into a resistance to *imperialism*. Similar movements took hold in China and southeast Asia.

On the Arabian Peninsula, Muhammad ibn Abd al-Wahhab offered his very strict interpretation of the Qur'an and *Sharia*, rejecting every innovation in Islam after the first three hundred years of the religion. He was particularly appalled by the worship of saints and a resurgence of tribal warfare on the Arabian Peninsula, and he called for a return to Islamic faith and practice as set forth by Muhammad and his companions in Medina. Al-Wahhab joined forces with a powerful tribal chief, Muhammad ibn Saud. Together, they conquered Arabia, spreading Wahhab's brand of Islam and creating the foundations for the modern state of Saudi Arabia.

Other Islamic thinkers attempted to deal with the reality of Islamic interaction with Western societies. They sought to develop ways to incorporate modern practices into Islam. By the 19th century, this would lead to the first wave of Islamic modernism, in which people argued that Islamic faith was not incompatible with new advances in technology and science, and that modern Western methods of intellectual inquiry could successfully be combined with the Muslim faith. Throughout the Muslim world, modernist thinkers banned together to study and promote their ideas as a way to ensure continued political and cultural relevance for Islam.

As European colonial powers exerted more and more control over the Muslim world, Muslim *nationalism* also took hold. Independence movements in numerous countries sought freedom from foreign rule and devoted themselves to developing their own national governments primarily based on Western notions of national government. After the end of World War I, the Ottoman Empire was dissolved. The new state of Turkey established a secular government in which church and state were separate. In Persia (renamed Iran in 1935), although the monarchy remained, new leaders sought to create a secular state system similar to those of the West. The colonial powers took over former Ottoman territories in the Arab world. Although some, like Egypt, Syria, and Iraq, eventually gained independence, their governments remained closely tied to the European powers.

In the period after World War II, as European colonialism gradually came to an end, some countries aligned themselves with more democratic traditions (such as Turkey, Tunisia, and the newly formed Pakistan) while others took a more socialist stance (such as Egypt, Syria, Iraq, Libya, Algeria, Yemen, and Indonesia). These nationalist movements did not lock Islam out of the picture; rather, they allowed for the influence of Islam in society, but they did not enforce Islamic law or make it a key feature of their governments.

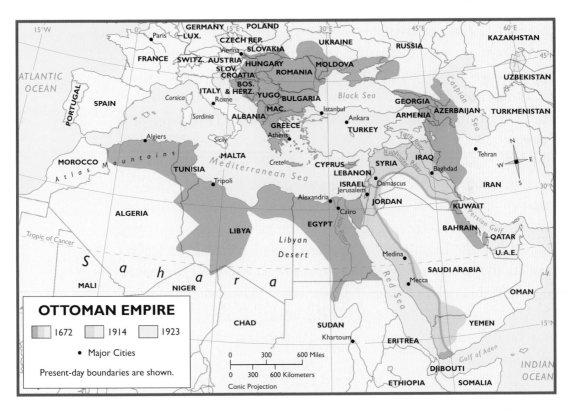

For hundreds of years the Ottoman Turks ruled over a vast and powerful empire. At its height in the 16th and 17th centuries the empire included large parts of North Africa, the Arabian Peninsula, Central Asia, and Eastern Europe. By the start of World War I in 1914, however, the weakened Ottoman empire was ridiculed as the "sick man of Europe." The Ottomans entered the war on the side of the Central Powers (Germany and Austria-Hungary); after the war was lost the Ottoman territories were carved up by the victorious Allied powers (in particular, France and Great Britain) and the modern state of Turkey was established in 1923.

In a handful of countries, such as Morocco, Jordan, Oman, and Malaysia, Islamic authorities legitimized monarchies. In other countries, like Saudi Arabia and Yemen, Islamic authorities still wielded real power.

CONTEMPORARY FUNDAMENTALISM AND MODERNISM

Most Muslim countries achieved independence during the 20th century, but many of the new nations did not prosper. Political systems failed and unfavorable economic conditions led to high unemployment and increasing levels of frustration among the poor. The process of modernization also eroded traditional values. As a result, fundamentalist groups condemned Western influences and sought to counter nationalist movements. Two influential Islamist groups were the Muslim Brotherhood, established in Egypt in 1928 by Hasan al-Banna (d. 1949), and the Islamic Society, founded by Mawlana Abu al-Ala Mawdudi (d. 1979) in India in 1941. These groups criticized both popular innovations within Islam and the secularism of the nationalists. Al-Banna argued that the Islam and the Qur'an offered everything Muslims needed; they did not need to turn to the West for ideas about how to govern themselves or run their societies. Mawdudi made much the same argument, and opposed the concepts of both socialism and capitalism. Both believed that Islamic law should apply to every area of life.

In the 1960s, the Egyptian Sayyid Qutb took the message of the Muslim Brotherhood further by declaring Western societies as *jahiliyya*, or barbaric due to a lack of Islamic rule. He called for *jihad* against rulers of secular Muslim societies, whom he considered corrupted by their associations with more powerful countries such as the United States. Qutb's views led to his execution in 1966, but his writings helped define contemporary Islamist ideas about revolution and the institution of Islamic governments.

The June 1967 War, in which Israel decisively defeated the combined forces of Egypt, Jordan, and Syria, ignited new feelings of outrage in Arabs who longed for the Islamic glories of the past. In 1973–74, the Arab states demonstrated their economic power to the West with an oil embargo that contributed to higher gasoline prices and hurt the U.S. economy. But the greatest success for the fundamentalists occurred with the Iranian revolution in 1979. Young militants forced the oppressive ruler of Iran into exile and swept the Shiite cleric Ayatollah Ruholla Khomeini and his supporters into power. Khomeini created a new Islamic republic in Iran, with a strict society that tightly controlled women, minorities, and opposition groups, and opposed Western and secular influences on Islam.

The Iranian revolution is the only significant example of extensive national reform on the part of fundamentalists in the last quarter of the twentieth century, though leaders like Libya's

The Shiite leader Ayatollah Ruholla Khomeini (1902–1989) rejected western culture and encouraged the establishment of a state in Iran founded on Islamic principles. The 1979 Iranian Revolution had an important effect on relations between the Muslim world and the West.

Muammar Qaddafi and Pakistan's General Muhammad Zia ul-Haq and opposition movements in Afghanistan, Egypt, Iran, and Saudi Arabia carried the banner of Islam to increase their legitimacy and popular support. In less radical approaches, students and the educated middle class worked for a gradual increase in Islamic influence. More militant groups, in contrast, believed that their national leaders were corrupt and that they should violently take power from sitting governments and impose a strict interpretation of the *Sharia*. These groups blamed not just their own leaders, but those of the West as well.

By the 1980s, the rise of Islamic fundamentalism and the success of the Iranian revolution inspired Muslims around the world to reassert their faith and place an increased emphasis on personal and community religious life. This included a renewed focus on observing Friday worship and the other Muslim holy days; developing Islamic information outlets, from television to radio to books; and forming Muslim political parties committed to Islamist reforms.

As a result, Islamic political organizations became an even more important part of the political process in Muslim countries in the 1980s and 1990s. Islamists successfully participated in elections in Turkey, Malaysia, Indonesia, and other countries. Though their concerns remained mostly domestic, Islamists made themselves heard on international issues as well, such the conflict between Israelis and Palestinian Arabs, the invasion of Afghanistan by the Soviet Union, United Nations sanctions against Iraq following the Persian Gulf War, and repressive efforts against Muslims in Bosnia, Chechnya, and Kashmir.

Beginning in the 1980s, small militant fundamentalist groups also began to proliferate, demanding total obedience to Allah in every aspect of life and asserting their religious duty to commit *jihad* against their oppressors. To defend their cause, these groups were willing to take up arms and resist their opponents in their own countries and elsewhere. Among them are Hizb Allah (Hezbollah, or "party of God"), a Shiite political force in

Lebanon; Hamas, which promotes Palestinian nationalism; and Islamic Jihad, a Palestinian group with close ties to Iran.

Though they comprise only a small minority of Muslim fundamentalists, the threat that violent groups pose to military forces and everyday citizens have unfortunately led many in the West to adopt the stereotype of all Islamist activists—and sometimes even all Muslims—as violent.

Debris marks the site of the U.S. Marine headquarters and barracks building in Beirut, Lebanon that was destroyed in a terrorist attack in October 1983, killing 241 U.S. marines. The group Hizb Allah, which carried out this attack and others against Western targets in Lebanon during the 1980s, justified its actions as self-defense against oppression from invaders.

It is crucial to review this history of fundamentalism and modernism in Islam before one can understand the intricate realities of contemporary Muslim life. Many people in the West have developed stereotypes of Muslims as being violent, oppressive of women, and anti-Western. But the realities are much more complicated. A closer look at two hotly debated issues within Islam today—the rights of women and Muslim attitudes toward non-Muslims—are helpful to understanding the complex and varied views of Muslims around the world.

WOMEN AND THE VEIL

One of the primary images many Westerners have of Muslims is that of a Muslim woman covered except for her eyes and hands and secluded from public life. These two practices are known as veiling and *purdah*.

Veiling takes several forms. The *hijab* is a headscarf that sometimes includes a veil covering all of the face except the eyes. A *chador* is a loose, typically black robe that covers the body and most of the face. The most complete veiling is called a *burqa*; it covers the entire body from head to toe, with only a mesh grid over the eyes through which to see. The *hijab* is the most common of the three.

None of these garments is specifically prescribed in the Qur'an. Rather, the Muslim holy text calls simply for modesty:

> And say to the believing women that they should lower their gaze and guard their modesty; that they should not display their beauty and ornaments except what (must ordinarily) appear thereof; that they should draw their veils over their bosoms and not display their beauty except to their husbands. . . (Qur'an 24:31)

Qur'an 24:30 also calls for modesty among men, and the early Muslim women did not wear veils. But as Islam spread into Byzantine and Persian territories, Muslims began to adopt these cultures' practices regarding women's dress, which included veiling among upper-class women. Two hundred years after Muhammad's

A Muslim woman wears a headscarf that covers everything but her face. Many Muslim women do not view their religion's requirements for veiling to be oppressive.

lifetime, Islamic scholars interpreted the Qur'anic command to women to "draw their veils over their bosoms" to mean that women should cover their hair, neck, and ears. Muslim women did not commonly begin veiling themselves until around the tenth century.

The term *purdah* broadly refers to the practice of secluding women in public through the various types of veiling, but it also refers more specifically to segregating the sexes by keeping women in seclusion at home behind a high wall, curtain, or screen. The latter type of seclusion is not practiced by all Muslims, but is particularly prevalent in India (where some Hindus also follow this practice). The practice was probably adopted from the Persians after Muslims conquered the Persian Empire.

The original intent of these forms of seclusion was to shield women from unwanted advances from men and thus to protect their honor, but the laws about women's behavior and dress stiffened through time, and many women found that they were effectively cut off from community life. While rural women adopted the practices of veiling and *purdah* more slowly than their upper-class counterparts in the cities, once they were fully secluded they found themselves confined to small homes with very little outside contact. Any economic independence they had previously enjoyed was taken away, and all they knew of the public realm

Two women in burkas protest against a 2003 ruling by Germany's highest court that states can pass laws that outlaw religious dress in public schools. The sign worn by the woman on the left reads, "The forbidden face."

was what their male relatives were willing to tell them.

Veiling became an issue with the rise of modernism in the late 1800s. Modernist thinkers and reformers condemned the idea of women's protective clothing. For them, the veil symbolized the exclusion of women from public life during an era when women around the world, and particularly in the West, were finding more freedoms. Later, nationalists encouraged women to free themselves of their veils as a sign to colonizers that Muslim nations had adopted modern ways and were therefore ready to govern themselves. Although many women continued to wear whatever form of veil was traditional in their culture, some who refused began to advance the cause for broader rights for women in other areas of life—public worship, the family, and the workplace.

With the rise of modern fundamentalism came a renewed emphasis on the segregation of women. After the revolution in Iran, the new government under Ayatollah Khomeini instituted increased segregation of men and women in schools and at public events and restricted the types of work women could do outside the home. In addition, Iranian legal scholars viewed wearing a veil as a commandment from Allah and strictly enforced the practice; the government formed patrols to fine women who wore makeup or did not wear their veil in public. Perhaps the most extreme example of the imposition of the veil, however, occurred in Afghanistan when a group called the Taliban came to power in the mid-1990s. Afghani women were forced to wear *burqas*, could not work, and were forbidden to leave their homes unless accompanied by a male relative. The punishment for any failure to comply could include anything from fines to public execution.

But these are extreme examples. In general, veiling cannot be considered an oppressive practice forced on women by fundamentalist regimes. In recent years there has been a renewed interest among women throughout the Muslim world in wearing a veil as a sign of their commitment to Islam. Though veiling had been declining for some time in countries like Iraq, Syria, Lebanon, and Jordan, the practice has increased again.

Ironically, as women are granted new freedoms to work and attend universities, the veil provides them with some protection from male harassment. In the United States and Europe, some Muslim women wear a veil, while others do not.

Some sociologists and anthropologists have argued that the practice of wearing a veil has become a means of expressing dissent and opposition to secular governments in the Muslim world, and to social pressures that demand greater levels of Westernization and that dilute the people's sense of an Islamic identity. By wearing a veil, these experts say, women reassert their Islamic identity in response to the strong forces of Westernization.

With the fall of the Taliban in Afghanistan in 2001, the only other country besides Iran to mandate veiling is Saudi Arabia. By Western standards, Saudi Arabia's government is very conservative—women cannot travel without a man's permission, work in an occupation with men who are not relatives, pray in mosques, or drive a vehicle. However, women in Saudi Arabia have many other freedoms—they are increasingly well-educated and some lead full professional lives. In Iran today, more women are in the workforce than before the revolution and female students now outnumber male students in Iranian institutions of higher learning.

Islam incorporates diverse women with diverse views. Some women oppose any kind of segregation, while others accept the veil for spiritual or practical reasons but argue for increases in other rights. Some Muslim women are critical of state-enforced practices they view as oppression, while others defend their government's restrictions on women.

ATTITUDES TOWARD NON-MUSLIMS

Another issue highlighted by the contradictions between fundamentalism and modernism is Muslims' attitudes toward non-Muslims. Under Muhammad and his earliest successors, Islam was tolerant toward people who professed other religions; the Muslims were particularly tolerant of Jews and Christians, the "people of the book." This tolerance was tested repeatedly as the centuries passed, both as Islam spread east and west and when Western powers challenged the Muslim world, first during the Crusades and later during the era of European colonization.

Muslims modernists of the late 1800s and the 1900s saw favorable relations with non-Muslims as necessary to their efforts to assimilate Islamic societies with Western ideas about science, secular education, and the separation of religion and government.

Fundamentalist Muslim leaders, however, seek to distance their followers from non-Muslim political and cultural ideas. Since the Islamists' vision of Islam is all-encompassing—it governs every part of society and personal life—outside influences are usually suspect. As Western culture has become more globally pervasive, Islamists try to shield Muslims from outside influences. To this end, they often portray the West as morally and culturally bankrupt and accuse Westerners of attempting to weaken Islamic institutions. Fundamentalists assert that a completely Islamic system is superior to capitalism, socialism, or any other kind of political structure.

Some extremists actually declare *jihad* against non-Muslims and resist their presence and influence by using violence. The attacks on the World Trade Center in 1993 and 2001; bombings at U.S. embassies in Kenya and Tanzania in 1998; and other widely publicized acts of terrorism have led to the notion that all Muslims are violent. But a closer look at the word *jihad* reveals that its root meaning is "struggle," and Muslims have traditionally interpreted the word to describe the many different ways one can practice Islam in the face of resistance. The "greater *jihad*" is the struggle within each Muslim to live a moral life. The "lesser *jihad*" refers to warfare or fighting against injustice. Most Muslims consider violence a last resort in the struggle against external forces.

The idea of using force to coerce unbelievers to embrace Islam, or to punish them for not accepting the faith, is rejected by Islam and most Muslims. Qur'an 2: 256 says, "Let there be no compulsion in religion," and Muhammad taught that to Allah, a forced conversion is worthless—such behavior on the part of a Muslim is

An FBI photograph of Osama bin Laden, who has been responsible for many devastating attacks on the United States. The U.S. State Department calls him "one of the most significant sponsors of Islamic extremist activities in the world today." Most Muslims reject the violent methods employed by bin Laden and other extremists.

a sin, and the person who converts to Islam because he fears for his life cannot truly be a Muslim. Thus, while many Islamists reject the Western worldview and political interference in the internal affairs of Islamic countries, and hope to extend the power and influence of Islam, they seek these changes through political processes rather than violence.

The rise of fundamentalism has affected how non-Muslims view Islam. Many people in the West see only images of terrorism on their television screens and stereotype the Muslims living among them as violent extremists who pose a threat to their secular societies. In many places around the world Muslims practice their religion every day while surrounded by people who do not understand the history or teachings of Islam. The tension between non-Muslim majorities and the Muslims living among them has at times broken into violence, in countries from Bosnia to India. Even in the United States, Muslim Americans found themselves the object of violence after the

September 11, 2001, terrorist attacks that destroyed the World Trade Center and damaged the Pentagon.

But in the United States, and in many countries of Europe, Muslim minorities are free to practice Islam, and the tensions are more cultural than religious. In the wake of the terrorist attacks in the United States on September 11, 2001, non-Muslim American citizens have shown great interest in learning more about and living peacefully alongside their Muslim counterparts.

Chronology

610   Muhammad receives the first revelations from Allah, which will later be recorded in the Qur'an.

613   Muhammad begins publicly preaching Allah's message.

622   Muhammad and his followers begin the *hijra*, or migration, from Mecca to Medina, an event that marks the beginning of the Muslim era.

630   An Arab Muslim army led by Muhammad takes control of Mecca.

632   Muhammad dies, and the era of the "rightly guided caliphs" begins when Abu Bakr is chosen as the first caliph.

656   Ali becomes the fourth caliph, sparking a civil war in the Muslim community.

661   Ali is assassinated, and Muawiyya declares himself caliph. Ali's supporters, the Shiites, continue to support his sons' claim to the caliphate.

680   Ali's son Hussein is killed, with his family and many supporters, at the Battle of Karbala.

683   The Umayyad succession of caliphs begins. Based in Syria, their rule extends eastward to the borders of India and China and westward to Spain.

749   The Abbasids overthrow the Umayyads.

820   al-Shafii, who created an authoritative methodology for developing *Sharia*, dies.

874   The power of the Abbasid caliphs begins to wane; local dynasties start to establish rule throughout the Abbasid empire.

1058   The jurist and mystic al-Ghazali is born; he eventually helps make Sufism accepted by mainstream Islam.

Chronology

1099 The European Crusaders capture Jerusalem and establish four Crusader kingdoms.

1187 Muslim forces under Saladin defeat the Crusaders and recapture Jerusalem.

1453 The armies of the Ottoman Turks capture Constantinople, bringing the thousand-year rule of the Byzantine empire to an end.

1502 The Safavid Empire is established in Iran; Shia Islam becomes the state religion.

1526 The Moghul Empire is founded in India.

1765 Great Britain forces the Moghul emperor to give up control of part of India; the British will eventually control all of the area of modern-day India and Pakistan.

1919 In the conference that ends World War I, the Arab lands of the defeated Ottoman empire are divided into small states and placed under the control of France or Great Britain.

1923 Turkey establishes the first secular government in a Muslim country.

1928 Hasan al-Banna founds the Muslim Brotherhood in Egypt.

1941 Mawlana Abu al-Ala Mawdudi establishes the Islamic Society in India.

1947 Pakistan is created as an Islamic state.

1948 Israel is founded, and immediately fights a two-year war for independence with its neighbors.

1967 Israel defeats the combined forces of Egypt, Jordan, and Syria in the Six-Day War.

Chronology

1978 U.S. President Jimmy Carter helps to negotiate a historic peace treaty between Israel and Egypt.

1979 Revolution grips Iran and the Islamic Republic comes to power.

1980 Iraq invades Iran, setting off an eight-year conflict in the Persian Gulf.

1991 An international coalition of nations, led by the United States, attacks Iraq, forcing it to withdraw from Kuwait, which it had invaded and annexed in 1990.

1993 After secret negotiations in Oslo, Norway, representatives of Israel and the Palestinians establish a framework for an end to violence and the eventual establishment of an autonomous Palestinian state.

1995 During ethnic fighting in Bosnia, Serbian troops overrun a U.N. "safe area" at Srebrenica; an estimated 7,000 Muslim men and boys are massacred and buried in mass graves.

2000 The Israeli-Palestinian peace process fails, and the second *intifada* begins.

2001 On September 11, terrorists crash hijacked airplanes into the World Trade Center in New York and the Pentagon near Washington, D.C.; the U.S. responds by attacking Afghanistan and overthrowing the Taliban regime, which had sheltered the al-Qaeda terrorist network. This action is condemned by many Muslims.

2003 In March, the United States attacks Iraq to remove Saddam Hussein from power. Muslims and representatives of other countries criticize the attack.

Glossary

ablution—a cleansing of the body or parts of the body, particularly as a religious ritual.

alms—money, food, or other goods given as charity to the poor.

analogy—the logical assumption that if two things are shown to be alike in some ways, then they must be alike in other ways.

asceticism—denying oneself physical pleasures in the belief that this practice frees the body from material concerns and allows union with the divine.

caliph–"successor" or "deputy"; political leader of Sunni Muslims after the death of Muhammad.

colonialism—the practice of one country expanding to control one or more other countries, often with the goal of developing and maintaining an empire. This typically involves the belief that the values of the colonizing country are better than those of the colonized.

dowry—money, property, or a pledge of money or property given by a husband to his wife at the time of marriage.

Hadith–the report of a saying or action of Muhammad or one of his Companions.

imperialism—a system in which a country rules another country, either by directly occupying territory or by indirectly controlling political or economic processes.

jihad–struggle; the greater *jihad* refers to an individual's struggle to live a pure life; the lesser *jihad* refers to defensive struggle or warfare against non-Muslim aggression and influence.

Glossary

monogamy—the custom of having only one spouse at a time.

monotheism—belief in only one god.

mu'adhdhin—the mosque leader who issues the call to prayer at various times each day.

mysticism—the belief that one can experience direct union with the divine, especially through prayer and meditation; more generally, an emphasis in religion on feeling and faith rather than reason.

nationalism—a collective consciousness in which citizens emphasize the culture, interests, and political independence of their nation.

Passover—one of the most important Jewish holidays, commemorating the exodus of the Jews from Egypt and traditionally lasting for seven or eight days.

patriarchy—a social system in which the father is the head of the family, descent is traced through the male line, and men wield authority over women and children.

pilgrimage—a journey (often long and difficult) to a shrine or other place of religious significance.

polygyny—the custom of having more than one wife at a time.

polytheism—belief in more than one god.

Qur'an—the divine revelation that Muhammad received and recited to his followers. This is the holy book of Islam.

Ramadan—the ninth month of the Islamic lunar calendar, which is a period of meditation and self-sacrifice for Muslims.

secular—without any overt or specific relation to religion.

Glossary

self-flagellation—punishing oneself physically, especially by whipping.

Sufism—a mystical movement within Islam, through which Muslims seek a closer union with Allah.

Sunna—The example of Muhammad's life, as recounted in the Hadith.

ummah—The worldwide community of Muslims.

Zoroastrianism—religious system founded by Zoroaster and set forth in a holy text (the Avesta), which teaches the worship of a single god in the context of a universal struggle between good and evil. This was at one time the national religion of Persia.

Internet Resources

http://www.arches.uga.edu/~godlas/islamwest.html

Comprehensive collection of essays and links to online sources on Islamic history, culture, sects, law, and contemporary issues; also provides links to glossaries, maps, and online versions of the Qur'an and Hadith.

http://www.fordham.edu/halsall/islam/islamsbook.html

Links to texts from every period in the history of Islam; also includes a time-line covering the years 500–1999.

http://www.Quran.org

Links to Qur'an resources, including online translations, browsers, and commentary.

http://www.islamicity.com/

Background articles and recent news, with extensive audio and video resources on prayer, Ramadan, and *hajj*.

http://www.islamamerica.org/index.cfm

The website of Dar al Islam, a non-profit organization that promotes understanding between Muslims and non-Muslims in the United States. Includes recent news and academic articles on politics, culture, and history.

http://www.pbs.org/wgbh/pages/frontline/shows/muslims/

A special installment of the PBS program *Frontline* that examines contemporary Islam through profiles of and interviews with Muslims in the United States, Africa, the Middle East, and Asia.

Further Reading

Armstrong, Karen. *Islam: A Short History.* New York: Modern Library, 2000.

Asadd, Muhammad. *The Road to Mecca*. Louisville, Ky.: Fons Vitae, 2001.

Brooks, Geraldine. *Nine Parts of Desire: The Hidden World of Islamic Women*. New York: Anchor Books, 1996.

Chittick, William C. *Sufism*. Oxford, England: Oneworld Publications Ltd., 2000.

Cohen, Joshua and Ian Lague, eds. *The Place of Tolerance in Islam*. Boston: Beacon Press, 2002.

Renard, John, ed. *Windows on the House of Islam: Muslim Sources on Spirituality and Religious Life*. Berkeley: University of California Press, 1998.

Sells, Michael, translator. *Approaching the Qur'an: The Early Revelations.* Ashland, Ore.: White Cloud Press, 1999.

Seyyed, Hossein Nasr, Sewed H. Nasr, and Ali Kazuyoshi Nomachi. *Mecca the Blessed, Medina the Radiant: The Holiest Cities of Islam.* New York: Aperture, 1997.

Index

Numbers in **bold italic** refer to captions.

Index

Index

Index

Index

Picture Credits

Contributors

General Editor DR. KHALED ABOU EL FADL is one of the leading authorities in Islamic law in the United States and Europe. He is currently a visiting professor at Yale Law School as well as Professor of Law at the University of California, Los Angeles (UCLA). He serves on the Board of Directors of Human Rights Watch, and regularly works with various human rights organizations, such as the Lawyer's Committee for Human Rights and Amnesty International. He often serves as an expert witness in international litigation involving Middle Eastern law, and in cases involving terrorism, national security, immigration law and political asylum claims.

Dr. Abou El Fadl's books include *The Place of Tolerance in Islam* (2002); *Conference of the Books: The Search for Beauty in Islam* (2001); *Rebellion in Islamic Law* (2001); *Speaking in God's Name: Islamic Law, Authority, and Women* (2001); and *And God Knows the Soldiers: The Authoritative and Authoritarian in Islamic Discourse* (second edition, revised and expanded, 2001).

Dr. Abou El Fadl was trained in Islamic legal sciences in Egypt, Kuwait, and the United States. After receiving his bachelors degree from Yale University and law degree from the University of Pennsylvania, he clerked for Arizona Supreme Court Justice J. Moeller. While in graduate school at Princeton University, where he earned a Ph.D. in Islamic Law he practiced immigration and investment law in the United States and the Middle East. Before joining the UCLA faculty in 1998, he taught at the University of Texas at Austin, Yale Law School, and Princeton University.

General Editor DR. SHAMS INATI is a Professor of Islamic Studies at Villanova University. She is a specialist in Islamic philosophy and theology and has published widely in the field. Her publications include *Remarks and Admonitions, Part One: Logic* (1984), *Our Philosophy* (1987), *Ibn Sina and Mysticism* (1996), *The Second Republic of Lebanon* (1999), *The Problem of Evil: Ibn Sina's Theodicy* (2000), and *Iraq: Its History, People, and Politics* (2003). She has also written a large number of articles that have appeared in books, journals, and encyclopedias.

Dr. Inati has been the recipient of a number of awards and honors, including an Andrew Mellon Fellowship, an Endowment for the Humanities grant, a U.S. Department of Defense grant, and a Fulbright grant. For further information about her work, see www.homepage.villanova.edu/shams.inati.

KIM WHITEHEAD is a writer, editor, and teacher. She has worked with numerous religious non-profits and holds an M.Div. and a Ph.D. in religion and literature. She lives in Mississippi with her husband and son.